MODALITY IN SPANISH AND COMBINATIONS OF MODAL MEANINGS

DANA **KRATOCHVÍLOVÁ**

KAROLINUM PRESS

PRAGUE 2018

KAROLINUM PRESS
Karolinum Press is a publishing department of Charles University
Ovocný trh 560/5, 116 36 Prague 1, Czech Republic
www.karolinum.cz

Layout by Jan Šerých
Set and printed in the Czech Republic by Karolinum Press
First English edition

This work was supported by the European Regional Development Fund-Project "Creativity
and Adaptability as Conditions of the Success of Europe in an Interrelated World"
(No. CZ.02.1.01/0.0/0.0/16_019/0000734).
This book was supported by the Charles University project Progres Q10, Language in the shiftings
of time, space, and culture.

A catalogue record for this book is available from the National Library of the Czech Republic.

The original manuscript was reviewed by Miroslava Aurová, Ph.D. (University of South Bohemia
in České Budějovice), and Dr. Tomás Jiménez Juliá (Universidad de Santiago de Compostela).

ISBN 978-80-246-3869-0
ISBN 978-80-246-3904-8 (pdf)

CONTENTS

LIST OF ABBREVIATIONS

cond.	conditional
e	seme of evaluation
ind.	indicative
LE	lexical expression of evaluation
LP	lexical expression of potentiality
LR	lexical expression of reality
LV	lexical expression of will
m	choice of mood
MM	modal meaning
MME	modal meaning evaluative
MMI	modal meaning interrogative
MMP	modal meaning potential
MMR	modal meaning real
MMV	modal meaning volitive
p	seme of potentiality
P	potentiality of a whole utterance
pres.	present tense
prob.	probabilitive
R	reality of a whole utterance
subj.	subjunctive
v	seme of will

ACKNOWLEDGMENTS

This book is a result of several years of study of the Spanish modal system. Its creation was a long process and I couldn't have finished it without the help and support of my professors and colleagues who have shared with me their understanding of the Spanish modal system and, more importantly, their interest in how Spanish works.

I would like to thank to Zuzana Nejedlá, my first professor of Spanish, who introduced me to the magical universe of Romance languages and stimulated my interest in their future study.

A great deal of my current vision of the Spanish verbal system and my approach to it is based on theories of two great linguists, Bohumil Zavadil and Petr Čermák from the Faculty of Arts of Charles University. I consider myself privileged for having had the opportunity to attend their classes and learn from them. This book is based on the concept of modality created by Bohumil Zavadil and I hereby express my gratitude to him for personal consultations that have helped me to understand his way of seeing the modality.

I am proud to have been a student of Petr Čermák, my professor of Spanish phonetics, morphology and syntax, tutor of both my diploma and Ph.D. thesis, my colleague at the Department of Romance Studies at the Faculty of Arts and, most importantly, my friend. I thank him for countless interesting classes, advice, his support and patience, making me feel welcome at the Department of Romance Studies and for creating a pleasant working environment that helped me finish this work.

Special thanks belong to the reviewers of this monograph, Miroslava Aurová and Tomás Jiménez Juliá. Miroslava Aurová from the University of South Bohemia was also one of the reviewers and one of the first readers of my Ph.D. dissertation that this monograph is largely based on. Her insights and observations have helped me prepare this "version 2.0" and helped me rethink and formulate better some of my original ideas. Tomás Jiménez Juliá from the University of Santiago de Compostela was the first foreign reader of this book and his commentaries helped me appreciate some important aspects of how Spanish native speakers understand the modality of their native language. I cannot thank both reviewers enough for their advice and for all the time and attention they dedicated to my book.

Finally, I express my personal thanks to my family. To Graeme Sheard, who kindly revised the whole manuscript from the point of view of an English native speaker, to my aunt and to my mom who have always supported me unconditionally. Without their help I could never have finished my study, dedicate myself to Spanish linguistics and become who I am.

November 2017, Prague

PREFACE

This work is dedicated to the analysis of Spanish modality, more concretely, of those areas where several types of modality (later we will use the term *modal meanings*) combine. These areas can be found at all levels of the Spanish modal system; however, they are usually not systematically analysed in works about modality. We aim to study concrete cases where two modal meanings appear at the same time (for example, expressions where personal evaluation combines with speaker's uncertainty or with his will) and situations where one modal meaning gradually changes into another (gradual expressions of reality / potentiality). Our goal is to prove that these areas form a natural part of the Spanish modal systems and are essential for its functioning. The analysis of ways in which several modal meanings combine should also present in a new light some crucial questions regarding the mood selection in Spanish (mainly the opposition indicative / subjunctive).

This work is based on the theoretic concept of Spanish modality formulated by Bohumil Zavadil. In this point, it differs from most works about modality, since we do not use universal terms such as *epistemic*, *deontic* or *root modality*. We do not intend to underestimate the role of universal concepts of modality, however, we believe that for a detailed analysis of concrete areas of Spanish modality, these concepts are not sufficient.

Bohumil Zavadil has presented some key aspects of his modality concept in four Spanish written articles (1968, 1975, 1979a, 1979b) and as a part of a Spanish written monograph about Spanish syntax (Zavadil – Čermák 2008). However, the most coherent presentations of his concept can be found in monographs written in Czech: a monograph about modality (Zavadil 1980) and as a part of a complex grammar of Spanish (Zavadil – Čermák 2010). Since Zavadil's most important contributions to the study of modality are only accessible to readers with good knowledge of the Czech language, the present monograph also aims to present Zavadil's theory to a wider public and point out the possibilities of its use when describing with detail the modality of a concrete language. For this reason, this book (even though it is mainly aimed for linguists interested in Spanish), does not require knowledge of Spanish or Czech from the reader, we provide English translation for all Spanish or Czech quotations (originals are given in footnotes) and translations of all the Spanish constructions that will be analysed.

1.

INTRODUCTION

1.1 MODALITY IN LANGUAGE

It is not easy to define clearly the area of modality, since different authors do not approach it in the same way. In our understanding, modality is a language category that is closely related to the psyche of a speaker and his subjectivity, we define it as **the way in which speaker's personal attitude regarding the content of his utterances is encoded in a concrete language**.

The great amount of works that, directly or marginally, analyse the problems related to modality offers a wide scale of opinions, inspiring insights and theoretical grounds, on the other hand it also leads to terminological and methodological instability.

1.1.1 MODALITY IN LOGIC AND FORMAL SEMANTICS

The category of modality has its roots in logic, however, the relationship between them can be understood in different ways. The original logical criteria are most strictly applied in the concepts formulated by formal semanticists (Lyons: 1986 [1977], Kratzer: 1991, Portner: 2009, Rubinstein: 2012). Angelika Kratzer (1991: 639) defines modality as an area that "has to do with necessity and possibility." Necessity and possibility are represented in English trough the modals *must* and *can*, between them, there are other modal words that are analysed through the semantics of possible worlds. In Romance modality, Kratzer's concept is used for example by Borgonovo – Cummins (2007) for the analysis of Spanish and French modal verbs.

We fully respect the importance and the contribution of formal approaches to modality, however, such a strong union between language and logic is not appropriate for the targets we wish to accomplish. In our understanding, language modality is directly related to the speaker's attitude and subjectivity, external conditions, including truth conditions that have their place in logically based approaches, do not play any role in our analysis.

When applying the logically based concepts to Spanish, we encounter also another problem: their strong connection to analytic resources for expressing modality. This can be observed for example with González Vázquez (2002) who applies a purely logical concept of modality to Spanish. Her study includes only modal verbs and adverbs and it is, therefore, reduced to the analysis of concrete modalizers that overshadow other ways of expressing modality, especially the verbal moods. In our understanding of modality, the choice of mood is one of the pillars of the Spanish modal system that cannot be left aside.

The role of subjectivity inside a logically based concept is strengthened by Declerck (2001). The author uses the term *t-world* which is "a world which is anchored to a given time *t*" (23), but he differentiates between objective and subjective *t-worlds*:

> An *objective t*-world is the unique real world that holds at a given time and which is judged real by an (imaginary) ideal outside observer viewing the world as it is at that given time. A *subjective t*-world is an alternative world which is not judged real by such an ideal outside observer but which is conceived of as real by some consciousness at a certain time. Such a *t*-world consists of the tensed (=anchored in time by their finite verb form) propositions that are deemed true by the world-creating consciousness at the given time. Thus, the situation referred to by *Amsterdam lies in Belgium* (which is counterfactual in the objective S-world[1]) actualizes in the counterfactual S-world existing in the mind of a speaker who is convinced that this assertion is true at S (23–24).

We prefer Declerck's understanding of modality also because of the wide range of expressions that can work as "nonfactual-world creating device" (25). The author uses the term *modalizers*[2] that comprises not only the traditionally mentioned modal auxiliaries and modal adverbs, but also:

> an intensional verb like *believe, suppose, imagine*, an attitudinal verb like *intend, want, hope, wish*, the subjunctive mood, the imperative mood, a conditional clause creating a 'theoretical world' [...], a tense auxiliary creating a future world (e.g. *will, be going to, be about to*) or expressing posteriority, an inserted comment clause with an intensional verb (e.g. *I think*), 'modal backshifting' [...] or 'modal conditionalization' or a combination of the latter two (28).

Our understanding of modality corresponds do Declerck's in some respects. We also see modality as an area where different language tools play their respective roles and can mutually affect each other, however, the position of the speaker and his subjective way of presenting events is still less salient in Declerck's concept which translates also into using terms such as *factual world* that refer to the truth condition and that are not relevant in our approach.

1.1.2 MODALITY IN COGNITIVE LINGUISTICS

In cognitive linguistics, modality has been treated in a rather different way. The focus was originally centred on the modals, gradually the problems regarding verbal moods have also become a topic.

---

1   S designates the speech time, *S-world* is: "a world that is anchored to S" (Declerck: 2011, 23).
2   We use the term *modalizer* too, however, our definition is narrower, we use it only for lexical expressions of modality, we do not refer to verbal moods as to modalizers.

In cognitive linguistics, modals are approached as so-called *grounding expressions*. These expressions (together with others such as articles, demonstratives or tense markers) allow the speaker to be implicitly present in an utterance (*construal* in cognitive terms). The level of implicitness the speaker incorporates himself with into a construal (without being present explicitly, for example via the use of personal pronouns) translates into the level of *subjectification* (see Langacker 1991a, 1991b, 2003). The terms *subjectivity* and *objectivity* are, therefore, understood in a more specific way than generally.

While this book is not based on cognitive linguistics, we prefer the cognitive approach to the formal one, especially due to the emphasis on psychological (rather than logical) aspects of language and communication in general. Readers interested in purely cognitive approaches to modality can refer to Langacker (1991a, 1991b, 2003) or Traugott (2007, 2011) (for a rather different understanding of subjectification), a comprehensive Czech summary of their theories can be found in Kanasugi (2013). Cognitive approach to selected aspects of Spanish modality is represented by Maldonado (1995), Achard (2000), Vesterinen – Bylund (2013) or Vesterinen (2014). Didactic aspects of a cognitive approach to the Spanish subjunctive are analysed by Ruiz Campillo (2004, 2006, 2008).

1.1.3 MODALITY FROM A CROSS-LINGUISTIC PERSPECTIVE AND UNIVERSAL CONCEPTS

There cannot be much discussion regarding the most influential work that presents modality from the cross-linguistic point of view and concentrates on its manifestations in different languages. The monograph *Mood and Modality* by Frank Palmer (1986, second edition 2001) has been generally accepted as a fundamental work in this area that demonstrates how modality behaves in languages around the world.

In the original concept presented in the first edition (1986), Palmer distinguishes between two basic types of modality: *Epistemic* and *Deontic* that have their respective subtypes (*Declaratives*, *Judgments*, *Evidentials* and *Interrogatives* as parts of the Epistemic modality and *Directives*, *Commisives*, *Volitives* and *Evaluatives* as parts of the Deontic sphere). In the updated edition from 2001, Palmer changes somewhat the original schema and recognizes also the *Dynamic modality* which, together with the Deontic one, constitutes the basis of the *Event modality*.[3] The main difference between Dynamic and Deontic modality is resumed in the following way:

---

3   In similar contexts, other authors (including Declerck 2001 whose work we mentioned above) prefer the term *Root modality* that has been gaining importance especially since the publication of *The Semantics of the Modal Auxiliaries* by Coates (1983) and is probably more extended nowadays than Event modality.

In the simplest terms the difference between them is that with deontic modality the conditioning factors are external to the relevant individual, whereas with dynamic modality they are internal. Thus deontic modality relates to obligation and permission, emanating from an external source, whereas dynamic modality relates to ability or willingness, which comes from the individual concerned (Palmer 2001: 9).

Palmer's work presents a coherent concept of modality as a language category and the inventory of basic types of modality is presented as universal. Palmer's approach to modality is close to ours due to the wide range of its manifestations that the author recognizes. Nevertheless, for a complex and detailed description of subtle modal nuances that can be found in one concrete language, we consider the universal typology limiting and not sufficiently precise. For an extended discussion regarding the problems resulting from applying Palmer's concept to Spanish, Italian and Romanian, see Kratochvílová (2014).

An influential and coherent universal concept of modality was also presented by the American linguist Joan Bybee (compare, Bybee – Perkins – Pagliuca 1994). Even though her approach has not gained as much success as the Palmer's one, it has still been used by some linguists (recently, for example, by Nordström 2010). This concept does not use the terms deontic and dynamic modality, it complements the epistemic modality with the following types: *agent-oriented modality*, *speaker-oriented modality* and *subordinating modality*. While agent-oriented modality relates to an objectively apprehended obligation, necessity, ability or desire, the speaker-oriented modality relates to subjective will and it contains *imperatives*, *prohibitives*, *optatives*, *hortatives*, *admonitives* (i.e. warnings) and *persmissives*. Modality expressed in subordinate clauses is analysed in the framework of subordinating modality.

While Bybee's concept presents an interesting tool for general descriptions of modality in different languages, we must again consider it insufficient for a detailed analysis of Spanish modality. This approach that combines semantic and syntactic criteria is not ideal for a complex analysis of the modality in Romance languages that have a wide range of uses of the subjunctive, i.e. a mood appearing predominantly in the subordinate clauses.

1.2 ZAVADIL'S APPROACH TO MODALITY

For our purpose of analysing specific areas of the Spanish modality we decided to work with a concept that is based solely on the modality of Spanish. Such a concept enables us to describe in detail subtle modal differences that are, however, morphosyntactically encoded in the language and have their formal manifestations.

This concept has its origins in the seventies when the author presented some of its aspects in several Spanish written articles (Zavadil 1968, 1975, 1979a, 1979b). In its complexity, the theory was coherently presented in a monograph dedicated to the Spanish modality written in Czech: *Kategorie modality ve španělštině* (*The Category of Modality in Spanish*, Zavadil 1980). This approach to modality also forms part of university text books *Současný španělský jazyk* (*Contemporary Spanish Language*, Zavadil 1995, published in Czech) and *Sintaxis del español actual* (Zavadil – Čermák 2008). An updated version of this approach was presented in *Mluvnice současné španělštiny* (*Grammar of Contemporary Spanish*, Zavadil – Čermák 2010, written in Czech). Recently, the author has adjusted his original concept so as to apply it to Catalan. The complex *Mluvnice katalánštiny* (*Grammar of Catalan*, in Czech) including a chapter dedicated to modality is due to be published in 2018.[4]

The key distinctive feature of Zavadil's concept is its profound anchoring in the Spanish verbal system. In this aspect, Zavadil's approach is similar to the theory of Veiga (1991) that is well known in Spanish linguistics. Unlike the universal approaches presented previously, this concept can be considered internal, i.e. formulated exclusively for Spanish and based on the specifics of its modal system. The author's theory does not refer to modal logic (not even on the terminological level), the concept can be defined as psychologically-linguistic and it is based on structural linguistics, especially on Charles Bally's theory (1965 [1932]).

This crucial aspect of Zavadil's theory can be seen both as the main advantage or disadvantage of the concept. Unlike with the external concepts provided by formal semantics, Palmer or Bybee, applying Zavadil's theory to languages other than Spanish requires great adjustments. As can be expected, the theory could be rather easily adapted for other Romance languages that display great structural similarities with Spanish (as has been, after all, proven by its recent application to Catalan). Since the basis of the theory is represented by morphosyntactic manifestations of speaker's attitude (especially the verbal moods), the basic concept could also be applied to languages with fusional verbal system, such as the Slavonic languages (the author was very well familiarized with Slavonic approaches to modality when formulating the first versions of his work). However, applying this theory to structurally different languages, including mostly analytic English or German, would be complicated and would require great changes in the very basis of the concept.

Nevertheless, the fact that the concept respects all structural features of Spanish enables us to create a very accurate description of modality in Spanish. It also provides a precise terminology that reflects even subtle modal nuances. This concept, thus, presents an ideal instrument for a profound analysis of Spanish modality. Since our main goal is to study precisely delimited areas within the Spanish modal system, we consider this concept the only possible tool for their exact description.

In summary, we believe that in present day research about modality, both external (or universal) and internal theories have their specific place. While an exhaustive analysis of the modality of one language should always be based on a concept that is suitable for the language and respects all its peculiarities, the universal concepts are

4   In this work, we cite the manuscript that was kindly granted to us by the author.

ideal for less profound contrastive analyses or observations about the nature of modality in general.

1.2.1 DESCRIPTION OF ZAVADIL'S CONCEPT

Zavadil's terminology does not use the terms *types of modality* or *modal flavours*, instead, it works with the so-called *modal meanings* (*significados modales* in Spanish, *modální významy* in Czech). According to the most up-to-date concept presented in the *Grammar of Contemporary Spanish* (Zavadil – Čermák 2010), there are five basic modal meanings that comprise the whole area of Spanish modality:

1) **Modal meaning real (MMR)**
   Represents the content of an utterance as coincident with reality.

2) **Modal meaning interrogative (MMI)**
   Represents the content of an utterance as a subject of an invitation to confirm or complete a piece of information.

3) **Modal meaning potential (MMP)**
   Represents the content of an utterance as imaginary.
   Subtypes:
   – proper potential
   – conditional (the realization of the content is impeded by some real or imaginary obstacle)
   – probabilitive (the veracity of the content is presented as probable or inferred)
   – of possibility (expression of an open possibility).

4) **Modal meaning volitive (MMV)**
   Represents the content of an utterance as a subject of subjective (imperative, desire, intention) or objective (necessity) will.
   Subtypes:
   – imperative (will is conceived as appellative, i.e. directed to an addressee)
   – desiderative (will is conceived as non–appellative)
   – optative (expression of a petition or a desire)
   – intentional (expression of an intention to do something)
   – of necessity (the realization of a process is presented as necessary).

5) **Modal meaning evaluative (MME)**[5]
   Represents the content of an utterance as a subject of evaluation.

---

5   Initially, the concept included also the *modal meaning declarative*, however this MM was later eliminated by the author and it belongs to the sphere of modal meaning real.

We shall now resume the crucial aspects in which Zavadil's concept differs from the universal concepts. As the author states, the ontological motivation for the modal meanings and for the category of modality in general can be found in the human psyche and its three main components: Intellect, Will and Emotions. The basic schema is the following one:

INTELLECT   ....   MM real / MM potential
↑   ....   MM interrogative
↓
WILL   ....   MM volitive
EMOTIONS   ....   MM evaluative

Image 1: Zavadil's schema of modality, from Zavadil – Čermák (2010: 249), the English translation is ours

The range of expressions of MMs is relatively large, Zavadil includes into the sphere of modality suprasegmental elements, lexical expressions and morphological elements, especially verbal moods. This way, the concept includes two kinds of modality that are traditionally distinguished by the Spanish tradition: *modalidad del enunciado* and *modalidad de la enunciación*. The first type refers the modality of an utterance, the second one refers to modality related to the formulation of an utterance (we might translate it as *modality of the speech-act*) and distinguishes types such as: declarative modality (*declarativa*), interrogative modality (*interrogativa*), imperative modality (*imperativa*), exclamative modality (*exclamativa*) or appellative (*apelativa*).[6] In Zavadil's approach, these two types are analysed together, enabling, thus, a better comprehension of the relationships between them.

1.2.2 VERBAL MOODS ACCORDING TO ZAVADIL

According to Zavadil, the core of Spanish modality is represented by verbal moods. In this respect the concept differs notably from the universal approaches (especially those based on logic and formal semantics) that emphasize primarily the modal verbs. According to Zavadil's concept, the Spanish modals such as *poder*, *deber* and *tener que* should be approached rather as a specific group of lexical expressions of modality that is present in the Spanish modal system, yet it is not the most important part of it.

The spectrum of verbal moods that the author distinguishes in Spanish is wider than the traditional one. While RAE (2009) operates only with three verbal moods: indicative, subjunctive and imperative, Zavadil recognizes the following set:

---

6   The set of types of *modalidad de enunciación* is not unanimous and varies according to the author, compare Otaola Olano (1988), Grande Alija (2002), RAE (2009).

Table 1: Spanish verbal moods according to Zavadil

Verbal mood	MMs it expresses	Paradigm	Example
Indicative	Real	HABLO	*Tiene razón.* (*He is right.*)
Imperative	Volitive imperative	¡HABLA!	*¡Ten cuidado!* (*Be careful!*)
Desiderative	Volitive desiderative	HABLE	*¡Que llueva!* (*May it rain!*)
Subjunctive	Potential Volitive Evaluative	HABLE	*Tal vez tenga razón.* (*He might be right.*) *Quiero que llueva.* (*I want it to rain.*) *Es bueno que llueva.* (*It is good that it rains.*)
Conditional	Potential conditional	HABLARÍA	*Tendría razón.* (*He would be right.*)
Probabilitive	Potential probabilitive	HABLARÁ	*Estará en casa.* (*He will be at home.*)

When referring to the desiderative and the probabilitive, Zavadil uses the term *parasite mood* that is based on the fact that these two verbal moods do not have their own paradigm, instead, they *parasite* on verbal forms that primarily express other moods or tenses.

The desiderative parasites on the paradigm of the subjunctive, the difference between them consists in the fact that the desiderative is used only in simple sentences while the subjunctive appears mostly in subordinate clauses. It also differs from the imperative by expressing non-appellative will while the imperative is always directed towards a listener. English does not possess a direct counterpart for this mood, however, a similar notion of non-addressed will in a simple sentence can be expressed via the (rather archaic) use of *may*: *¡Que llueva!* – *May it rain!*.

The probabilitive parasites on the forms of future indicative, in the past tense it parasites on the conditional. The sentence *Estará en casa* can have two possible interpretation:

a) *He will be at home* (in the evening, tomorrow, someday in the future...).

b) *I suppose he is at home* (I can see the light in his window, it is already late...).

Spanish grammar usually refers to this this kind of expressing probability as to epistemic uses of the future tense (see RAE 2009), however, the clearly modal character of the resulting utterance and the possibility of expressing the probability in different tenses (*Estará en casa: I suppose he is at home, Habrá estado en casa: I suppose he has been at home, Estaría en casa: I suppose he was at home, Habría estado en casa: I suppose he had been at home*), lead Zavadil to a reconsideration of the traditional approach and he presents the probabilitive as a fully-fledged member of the system of Spanish verbal moods.[7]

The main distinctive feature of the Spanish modality is, nevertheless, the subjunctive that has a wide range of uses. It is mostly used in subordinate clauses after expres-

---

7   This conclusion is also supported by the fact that the modal uses of the *habrá hablado* paradigm are more extended in nowadays language than its original temporal meaning of future perfect.

sions of will (for example, *querer: to wish, desear: to desire*) and personal evaluation (for example, *alegrarse: to be happy about something, molestar: to annoy*). It is also used after some expressions of uncertainty, especially when they are negated (for example, *no creo: I do not believe, no digo: I do not say*) or non-personal (for example, *es probable: it is possible, puede ser que: it may be that*). The subjunctive is also used in temporal clauses, especially in those that refer to future (*Llámame cuando tengas tiempo: Call me when you have*-subj. *time*), conditional and concessive clauses (*Si tuviera tiempo, te llamaría: If I had*-subj. *time, I would call you; Aunque tenga tiempo, no te llamaré: Even if I have*-subj. *time, I will not call you*), purpose clauses (*Te ayudo para que puedas terminar antes: I help you so you can*-subj. *finish sooner*) and relative clauses with non-concrete antecedent (*Necesito una secretaria que hable chino: I need a secretary that speaks*-subj. *Chinese*). The subjunctive can also appear in main clauses after adverbs that express uncertainty, here it can usually alternate with the indicative (for example: *Quizás sea / es cierto: Maybe it is*-subj. / ind. *true*).

The problems related to the use of the Spanish subjunctive have been widely analysed in Spanish linguistics and it is not our objective to treat them all here. For a summary of approaches to the Spanish subjunctive and extensive bibliography about this verbal mood, refer to Kratochvílová (2016). With reference to Czech, the Spanish subjunctive is analysed by Pamies Bertrán – Valeš (2015), with reference to Italian, an analysis of Romance verbal moods in contrast with English and Czech modal systems is presented by Klímová (2009).

Throughout this monograph we shall only analyse those aspects of the Spanish subjunctive that are closely related to the blending of two modal meanings.

1.2.3 SYNTACTIC LEVELS AT WHICH MODALITY CAN BE EXPRESSED

Zavadil distinguishes four syntactic levels at which modality is expressed:

a) **utterance**
   Ahora. (Now.)
   Probablemente ahora. (Probably now.)
   ¿Agua? (Water?)
   ¡Café! (Coffee!)

b) **simple sentence**
   Lo hace bien. (He does it well.)
   ¿Lo hace bien? (Does he do it well?)
   Lo haría bien. (He would do it well.)
   ¡Hazlo! (Do it!)
   ¡Ojalá lo haga! (May he do it!)
   Tal vez lo haga. (He might do it.)

c) **compound sentence**
   Te digo que lo hace bien. (*I tell you that he does it well.*)
   Te digo que lo hagas ya. (*I tell you to do it already.*)
   No creo que lo haya hecho. (*I don't think that he has done it.*)
   Me alegro de que lo hayas hecho. (*I am happy that you have done it.*)

d) **clausal modal constructions**
   Puede hacerlo bien. (*He can do it well.*)
   Prometo hacerlo bien. (*I promise to do it well.*)
   Déjame hacerlo. (*Let me do it.*)
   Quiero hacerlo. (*I want to do it.*)

This translates into the fact that both concrete ways of expressing modality and concrete modal meanings have different roles on these four syntactic levels.

In **utterances**, modality can be expressed only by suprasegmental and lexical features. The suprasegmental features can distinguish:
MM real:
Ahora. (*Now.*)
MM interrogative:
¿Ahora? (*Now?*)
MM volitive:
¡Ahora! (*Now!*)
MM evaluative:
¡¡¿Ahora?!! (*Now?!!*)
The lexical features can distinguish also the MM potential:
Quizás ahora. (*Maybe now.*)

In **simple sentences**, the morphological features come into play helping to distinguish:
MM real:
Lo hace bien. – indicative (*He does it well.*)
MM potential:
Tal vez lo haga. – subjunctive (*He might do it.*)
MM potential conditional:
Lo haría bien. – conditional (*He would do it well.*)
MM probabilitive:
Lo hará bien. – probabilitive (*He does it well, I suppose.*)
MM volitive imperative:
¡Hazlo! – imperative (*Do it!*)
MM volitive desiderative:
¡Que lo haga! – desiderative (*May he do it!*)

In **compound sentences**, for Spanish is prototypical the combination of lexical expressions of modality with the subjunctive in the subordinate clause. Zavadil introduces the term *congruential subjunctive* that we shall use as well. Uses of lexical expressions followed by the indicative or the subjunctive, give rise to:

MM real:

Estoy seguro de que lo hará. – indicative (*I am sure that he will do it.*)

MM proper potential:

No creo que sea cierto.[8] – subjunctive (*I don't believe that it is true.*)

MM potential of possibility:

Es posible que aparezca pronto. – subjunctive (*It is possible that he will appear soon.*)

MM volitive optative:

Te pido que lo hagas. – subjunctive (*I ask you to do it.* literally: *I ask you that you do it.*)

MM volitive intentional:

Intento que seas feliz. – subjunctive (literally: *I try that you are happy.*)

MM volitive of necessity:

Es necesario que nos vayamos. – subjunctive (*It is necessary that we leave.*)

MM evaluative:

Me alegro de que lo haya hecho. – subjunctive (*I am happy that he has done it.*)

Zavadil uses the term *modal part* for the main clause of these constructions (this term substitutes Bally's original term *modus* that might be confusing) and Bally's term *dictum* for the subordinate clause. The compound sentences that do not contain a lexical expression of will, evaluation or potentiality, yet they require the subjunctive are called indirectly modal and this type of use of the subjunctive is non-congruential according to Zavadil (*Vete antes de que te vean: Leave before they see*-subj. *you*; *Si pudiera, lo haría: If I could*-subj., *I would do it*; *Te lo digo para que te sientas mejor: I tell you this so you feel*-subj. *better*).

Clausal modal constructions are condensed constructions where the infinitive substitutes the subordinate clause. Any construction with a modal (*poder, deber, tener que, haber que*) is automatically a clausal modal construction. Nevertheless, when the subject of the modal part corresponds to the subject of the dictum, condensation is also possible with a wide range of other verbs. Clausal modal constructions give rise to several MMs:

MM real:

Dice saber la verdad. (*He claims to know the truth.*)

Jura protegerte. (*He swears to protect you.*)

MM proper potential:

Parece ser cierto. (*It seems to be true.*)

---

8   Zavadil classifies as utterances with MM potential only those subordinate clauses with a lexical expression of uncertainty that is followed by the subjunctive. In this point, we disagree with the author for we believe that a sentence like *Creo que es tarde* (*I believe it is*-ind. *late*) cannot be classified as expressing the MM real. We claim that the use of the subjunctive only strengthens the potentiality, but it does not create it entirely, for potentiality is already present in the verb *creer* (*to believe*). For an extended discussion about this topic, refer to Chapter 2.

MM potential of possibility:
Puedes sentarte. (*You can sit down.*)
MM volitive optative:
Te propongo verlo ahora mismo. (literally: *I propose to see him right away.*)
MM volitive intentional:
Decidió casarse. (*He decided to get married.*)
No pienso aceptarlo. (*I do not plan to accept it.*)
MM volitive of necessity:
Debes hacerlo. (*You must do it.*)
Hay que apurarse. (*One must hurry.*)
Tienes que salir. (*You have to leave.*)
Necesito decirte algo. (*I need to tell you something.*)
MM evaluative:
Siento verte tan triste. (*I am sorry to see you so sad.*)

1.2.4 SUMMARY OF ZAVADIL'S APPROACH TO SPANISH MODALITY

The following table presents a summary of Zavadil's concept of modality accompanied by examples for each syntactic level. Verbal moods corresponding to the morphological expression of each MM are underlined.

Table 2: Summary of Zavadil's approach to modality

Modal meaning	Utterance	Simple sentence	Compound sentence	Clausal modal construction	Morphologic expression
Real	*Más tarde.* (*Later.*)	*Es tarde.* (*It is late.*)	*Sé que es tarde.* (*I know it is late.*)	*Jura no llegar tarde.* (*He swears no to come late.*)	Indicative
Inter-rogative	*¿Más tarde?* (*Later?*)	*¿Es tarde?* (*Is it late?*)	*Me pregunto si es tarde.* (*I am asking myself whether it is late.*)	—	Indicative
Proper potential	*Tal vez más tarde.* (*Maybe later.*)	*Tal vez sea tarde.* (*Maybe it is late.*)	*No creo que sea tarde.* (*I don't think it is late.*)	*Parece ser tarde.* (*It seems to be late.*)	Subjunctive
Potential conditional	—	*Sería tarde.* (*It would be late.*)	—	—	Conditional
Potential probabili-tive	—	*Será tarde.* (*It is late, I suppose.*)	*Supongo que será tarde.* (*I suppose it is late.*)	—	Probabilitive
Potential of possibility	—	—	*Es posible que sea tarde.* (*It is possible that it is late.*)	*Puede ser tarde.* (*It can be late.*)	Subjunctive

Volitive imperative	—	¡Hazlo más tarde! (Do it later!)	—		(¿Quieres hacerlo más tarde, por favor?)[9]	Imperative
Volitive desiderative	—	¡Ojalá no sea tarde! (Hopefully it is not too late!)	—	—		Desiderative
Volitive optative	¡Más tarde! (Later!)	—		Te pido que lo hagas más tarde. (I ask you to do it later.)	Propongo hacerlo más tarde. (I propose to do it later.)	Subjunctive
Volitive intentional	—	—		He intentado que lo haga más tarde. (I have tried to get him to do it later.)	Intentaré hacerlo más tarde. (I will try to do it later.)	Subjunctive
Volitive of necessity	—	—		Es necesario que lo hagas más tarde. (It is necessary that you do it later.)	Tienes que hacerlo más tarde. (You have to do it later.)	Subjunctive
Evaluative	¡Tan tarde! (So late!)	—		Es una pena que sea tarde. (It is a shame that it is too late.)	Siento llegar tarde. (I am sorry to arrive late.)	Subjunctive

As can be observed, the modal meanings presented by Zavadil can find their (partial) correspondents in terms used by the universal concepts. The following schema presents the best candidates from logically based theories for each modal meaning, however, it is important to bear in mind that the correspondences are necessarily approximative. We also include specific (sub)types of modality mentioned by different authors.

Table 3: Zavadil's terminology vs. universal concepts

Zavadil's terminology	Universal concepts
MM real	Realis, Declaratives (Palmer 1986)
MM interrogative	Interrogatives (Palmer 1986)
MM potential	Epistemic modality, Extrinsic modality (Biber 1999), Irrealis Includes: Dynamic modality, Circumstantial modality, Judgements (Palmer 1986)
MM volitive	Deontic modality, Root modality, Intrinsic modality (Biber 1999) Includes: Bouletic (Boulomatic) modality (Rescher 1968), Symbouletic modality (Yanovich 2014)
MM evaluative	Evaluatives (Palmer 1986)

---

9   Zavadil analyses the interrogative constructions introduced by *querer* as transposed (and stylistically marked) expressions of the MM imperative (see Zavadil – Čermák 2010: 265). The literal translation of the example would be: *Do you want to do it later, please?*, however, the meaning is imperative (*Do it later, please!*).

As a summary, we may now resume the most important aspects of Zavadil's theory, especially those in which it differs from most universal concepts:

1) The author refuses logical approach to modality and centres his attention on the human psyche.
2) The theory was based upon an analysis of Spanish, i.e. it is defined for a concrete language.
3) The author does not identify the analysis of modality with the analysis of modal verbs, in his concept, there are three main ways of expressing modality: supraseg-mental, lexical and morphological features, he does not deny the influence of prag-matic features.
4) The core of the modal system is represented by verbal moods, the basic MMs are based on the functions of verbal moods in Spanish, not on the functions of modals.
5) The theory does not impede future broadening, throughout this work, we shall propose some minor adjustments or terminological specifications.

We consider these aspects crucial for a complex analysis of the Spanish modal sys-tem and we accept Zavadil's concept as an ideal basis for our analysis of areas where different types of modality, i.e. different modal meanings, blend and interfere.

1.3 EXPRESSIONS OF MODALITY

There is no general agreement regarding the range of expressions of the category of modality. These can be divided into four large groups:
1) suprasegmental features;
2) morphological features;
3) lexical features;
4) (hyper)syntactic and pragmatic features.
We claim that the position of these groups differs according to a concrete language and features typical for one language should not be automatically analysed in other languages. Regarding Spanish, we can resume the situation in the following way.

1.3.1 SUPRASEGMENTAL FEATURES

At the first place, we shall name the intonation that is crucial for the analysis of the above-mentioned *modalidades de la enunciación*. Zavadil also sees it as one of expres-sions of modality (he dedicates an extensive chapter to this topic in Zavadil 1980: 42–74).

1.3.2 MORPHOLOGICAL (MORPHOSYNTACTIC) FEATURES

In Spanish, the key morphological features are the verbal moods. Some authors also mention the prefixation and suffixation as another kind of morphological expression of modality that can be found mostly in non-Indo-European languages (see Palmer 1986, 2001). However, the role of these features inside the Spanish modal system is questionable. Brenner (2009) mentions the suffix -*ísimo* in this regard, we consider its modal interpretation as acceptable, however, it stands at the very edge of the Spanish modal system and the issue of modal suffixes and prefixes shall not be discussed in this work.

1.3.3 LEXICAL FEATURES

The transition between morphological and lexical expressions is represented by the modals that form the centre of the modal system of isolating languages such as English. Nevertheless, modals can also be found in languages with fusional verbal system such as Czech, Spanish or other Romance languages. The role of the modals within the Spanish modal system is analysed in Chapter 7.

Leaving aside the purely modal verbs, we might also consider the fully-semantic verbs and adverbs as lexical expressions of modality. These expressions are also related to the morphological expressions of modality due to the modal congruence with the subjunctive they might require (or enable).

We use the term *modalizers* to refer to these lexical expressions and to the proper modals. Modalizers and the problems of the modal congruence in the dictum are analysed throughout this whole book.

At the border between lexical and pragmatic features of modality are the so-called pragmatic markers (or pragmatic particles, *marcadores pragmáticos* in Spanish) that are analysed by Arce Castillo (1998) or Zavadil – Čermák (2008, 2010).

There are also other, more or less peripheral, lexical expressions of modality, however, their analyses are problematic and their position within the modal system remains unclear. Compare, in this respect, for example Franz (2009: 119) who studies the modal function of personal pronouns. As the author herself observes, "the analysis reveals that the interpretation of utterances with explicit subject pronouns depends on many aspects and it is, thus, not easy to prove the modalizing function of the pronoun."[10]

Some authors have also considered the modal function of conjunctions that stand between lexical and syntactic features. Compare Sweetser (1991), generally (but mainly with reference to Germanic languages) this topic is treated by Nordström (2010),

---

10 Original quotation (the translation is ours): "[e]l análisis muestra que la interpretación de enunciados con pronombres sujetos explícitos depende de numerosos aspectos y por lo tanto no es fácil comprobar una función modalizadora del pronombre."

for the analysis of Portuguese, see Blühdorn – Reichmann (2010), for Spanish, see Hummel (2004).

1.3.4 HYPERSYNTACTIC AND PRAGMATIC FEATURES

An approach that analyses the modality in the wider context of a discourse is in the Spanish linguistics defended, for example, by Pérez Sedeño (2001: 69), who presents the following arguments:

> We defend, thus, the modal phenomenon as discursive phenomenon in which the socio-cultural values of the speaker's tradition should be borne in mind, once considered this aspect, we defend an analysis that includes both the logical-semantic criteria and the pragmatic ones, depending on the concrete discourse.
>
> Modality is not a category or a concept that could be defined intentionally or extensionally, identifiable with a *grammatical word class*. On the contrary, it is a speech-act process belonging to the discourse that adopts different expressions depending on the communicative intentions of the speaker.[11]

1.4 OUR APPROACH TO MODALITY

1.4.1 THEORETICAL BASIS

The theoretical basis for our analyses is Zavadil's concept of modality. Unless stated otherwise, we accept his terminology and definitions as presented in the Chapter 1.2.

1.4.2 SYNTACTIC LEVELS

From the syntactic point of view, we shall concentrate on modality expressed in simple and compound sentences as well as in clausal modal constructions. However, we exclude from our research indirectly modal compound sentences where verbal moods have functions different to those in directly modal constructions and their use is often formalized (compare Zavadil – Čermák 2010: 266–270). Since the objective of our research is an analysis of relationships among modal meanings, it is impossible to anal-

---

11   Original quotation (the translation is ours): "Defendemos pues el fenómeno modal como fenómeno discursivo en el que han de tenerse en cuenta los valores socioculturales de la tradición en que se inscribe el enunciador y, considerado este aspecto, defendemos un análisis en el que quepan tanto los criterios lógico-semánticos como pragmáticos, según lo requiera el propio discurso. La modalidad no es una categoría o concepto que se pueda definir intesional o extensionalmente, identificable con ninguna *clase de palabras gramaticales*. Al contrario, es un hecho enunciativo que pertenece al discurso y que adopta expresiones diferentes en función de las intenciones comunicativas del enunciador."

yse the directly modal compound sentences together with constructions where these relationships are altered or disrupted.

1.4.3 EXPRESSIONS OF MODALITY

As stated above, modality is a complex category consisting of several levels that can be approached from different perspectives. Zavadil analyses mainly its suprasegmental, lexical and morphosyntactic features. We shall, with some adjustments, adopt this approach as well.

We do not include in our research the pragmatic dimension of this category (including the analysis of pragmatic markers). We consider conclusive the above-cited argument presented by Pérez Sedeño (2001) that modality should be understood (also) as a pragmatic category, nevertheless, we find it necessary to delimit this area to a certain extent in order to approach it methodologically. When analysing the modality from the point of view Pérez Sedeño suggests, this category becomes complex, yet, also, hard to analyse systematically.

We shall not analyse the suprasegmental features either, for they belong mostly to phonetics that is not our main area of interest.

We concentrate on the morphosyntactic features of this category, concretely on verbal moods, and we dedicate special attention to selected lexical features: verbal and adverbial modalizers, including the modal verbs. We consider these areas the core of the Spanish modal system that deserve the attention most.

1.4.4 METHODOLOGY

In the following chapters, we analyse separately different areas where two modal meanings meet. Our goal is to describe these areas and their role inside the Spanish modal system. In each chapter, we choose a concrete manifestation of a combination of two MMs in Spanish. This way, we aim to present a wide spectrum of concrete possibilities of combining two MMs and the consequences resulting from this combination. We do not exclude other possible combinations (some of them are also mentioned in the text). The selection of concrete representations of combining two MMs that will be subjected to analysis was based on the following criteria:

- frequency of use (we prefer frequently used constructions to less frequent ones)
- level of fixation (we prefer those constructions that are systemically encoded in the language and have a fixed structure)
- consequences of the combination of MMs (if possible, we choose those constructions where a combination of modal meanings has consequences on the mood selection).

In the chapters' headings, the relationship is represented by the symbol of arrow (→). The following six chapters have a chain structure, since one of the two MMs presented in the previous chapter is also analysed in the following one. This way, we aim to point out the inherently gradual character of modality. The organization of the following chapters is as follows:

MM real → MM potential (Chapter 2)
MM potential → MM evaluative (Chapter 3)
MM evaluative → MM volitive (Chapter 4)
MM volitive → MM interrogative (Chapter 5)
MM interrogative → MM potential (Chapter 6)
MM potential → MM volitive (Chapter 7)

When possible, theoretical analyses are combined with data obtained from language corpus. We work mainly with the parallel corpus InterCorp (www.korpus.cz/intercorp) that was created at the Charles University. The corpus contains texts in 40 languages, including Spanish and English. For a complex description of the corpus, refer to Čermák – Rosen (2012). Since the corpus contains several translations of one single text that can be simultaneously compared, it is ideal for contrastive analyses. For an exhaustive analysis of the possible employment of parallel corpora, see Nádvorníková (2016, 2017).

The corpus enables to use complex queries which were often indispensable in our analyses. In this aspect, the possibilities are considerably larger than those that offer the reference corpora created by RAE (CREA and CORPES XXI). These were used only in those cases where InterCorp could not provide sufficient volume of data.

We work with the version 9 of InterCorp available since 9th September 2016. This version contains a total of 1 647 million words in 40 languages, the complete Spanish subcorpus contains a total of 129 792 974 tokens. For our purposes, we created a considerably smaller subcorpus that contained only original Spanish texts (i.e. we excluded all Spanish translations from other languages). They are all literary texts, mostly written in the 20th and 21st century. Their list can be found in the Appendix 1. Our subcorpus contains a total of 11 962 162 tokens. When necessary, we divide this subcorpus into two parts: Hispano-American authors and Spanish authors. The Hispano-American part contains 7 990 788 tokens, the Spanish one is smaller and contains 3 971 374 tokens. Unless stated otherwise, all the analyses presented in this book are based on this subcorpus.

To ensure the examples from the corpus are also accessible to readers who do not speak Spanish, we have provided our own translation for all of them. Even though some of the books they are taken from have been translated to English, we decided to translate all the quotations by ourselves. The official translations would not serve our purposes properly, since they do not concentrate on the modal meanings expressed in Spanish, but rather on the general stylistics of the text. With each example, we seek to provide the most literal translation possible, maintaining the original modal meaning embedded in it. In some cases, this may result in somewhat unnatural translation, which we are well aware of, however, our main goal is to represent the discussed construction in English, reflecting, as much as possible, its original structure and illustrating, thus, how a concrete modal meaning is expressed in Spanish.

2. MODAL MEANING REAL → MODAL MEANING POTENTIAL

The first kind of relationship we are going to analyse, is the relationship between the modal meaning real (MMR) and modal meaning potential (MMP).[12] These modal meanings are closely connected, since they are both attached to the speaker's conviction regarding the veracity of his utterance: "The MM real characterises the content of an utterance as corresponding to reality, the MM potential characterises the content of an utterance as imaginary, i.e. existing only in form of an imagination" (Zavadil 1980: 24).[13]

The MMP has several subtypes; the MM potential probabilitive that "characterises the verbal process as probably realized" (Zavadil – Čermák 2010: 251)[14] and the MM potential conditional that "characterises the verbal process as imaginary (i.e. existing only in form of an imagination) and, at the same time, in this imagination dependent on the fulfilment of a certain condition. This condition can be either explicit (verbally expressed, named) or implicit (not expressed verbally)" (Zavadil – Čermák 2010: 251).[15]

Each above-mentioned MM can be linguistically expressed both in lexical or morphological form. MMR's verbal mood is the indicative (*Está trabajando*: He is-ind. *working*), the MMP probabilitive is grammatically expressed through the probabilitive (*Estará trabajando*: He is-prob. *working*), the MMP conditional corresponds to the use of the conditional (*Estaría trabajando*: He is-cond. *working*). Only in utterances with the MM potential (proper potentiality) there is a modal alternation between the subjunctive and the indicative (*Tal vez esté / está trabajando*).[16]

As can be seen from the previous definitions, different types of the MMP have also different kind of relationship to the MMR. For our purposes (i.e. an analysis of rela-

---

12　General observations made in this chapter have already been presented in a Spanish written article "Las relaciones entre el significado modal real y el significado modal potencial en español" published in *Linguistica Pragensia* n. 23 (Kratochvílová 2013b). However, this chapter presents a considerably extended version of this article, accompanied by a large series of corpus analyses that shed new light on the original topic.

13　Original quotation (the translation is ours): "MV reálný charakterizuje obsah výpovědi jako odpovídající skutečnosti, MV potenciální charakterizuje obsah výpovědi jako imaginární, tj. existující pouze v podobě představy."

14　Original quotation (the translation is ours): "charakterizuje děj predikátoru jako domněle nebo pravděpodobně realizovaný."

15　Original quotation (the translation is ours): "charakterizuje děj predikátoru jako imaginární (tj. jako existující v podobě představy) a zároveň v představě závislý na splnění nějaké podmínky. Tato podmínka může být explicitní (jazykově vyjádřená, pojmenovaná) nebo implicitní (jazykově nevyjádřená)."

16　As stated in Chapter 1.2.4, in this aspect we deviate slightly from Zavadil's original concept, since we do not consider the selection of the subjunctive as crucial for distinguishing between the MM real and the MM potential.

tionships between modal meanings), the most interesting situations are those where this relationship is not altered by any external factors and the degree of potentiality / reality of an utterance depends only on the degree of speaker's commitment. Therefore, for the existence of an external obstacle that impedes the fulfilment of the proposition, we will leave aside the MMP conditional. We also leave aside the MMP probabilitive. The relationship between probability and potentiality is accurately summarized by Jiménez Juliá (1989: 203-204):

> [T]he probability is related to "possibility," but they are not equal. They coincide on the general absence of certainty, but they present it differently. [...] An example can illustrate the difference between these two notions: if we ask for Antonio and our listener does not know where he is at the moment, he can reply:
> 8. Quizás esté en la biblioteca [(Maybe he is-subj. in the library)].
> In that case, what he is saying to us is that Antonio might be in the library or that he might not be there, since the library is a *possible* place to find him. There is, however, the possibility that he is somewhere else. This way, (8) corresponds to (can be substituted by) (9):
> 9. Es posible que Antonio esté en la biblioteca [(It is possible that Antonio is-subj. in the library)], which implies:
> 10. Es posible que Antonio no esté en la biblioteca [(It is possible that Antonio is-subj. not in the library)].
> Nevertheless, when the speaker not only admits this possibility, but he also has good reasons to believe that Antonio actually is in the library, even though he cannot be positive about it, he can reply:
> 11. Estará en la biblioteca [(He is-prob. in the library)].[17]

We agree with Jiménez Juliá on his interpretation of probability as a notion that comprises both speaker's commitment and certain external circumstances that lead to a conclusion regarding the presupposed state-of-facts. It is precisely the existence of those external conditions that impede us to analyse the MMP probabilitive together with the proper MMP.

Therefore, in this chapter, we will analyse solely those utterances that express the proper potentiality or reality, considering also the possibilities of their lexical expression. Selected issues regarding the Spanish probabilitive will be analysed in Chapter 6.

---

17   Original quotation (the translation is ours): "[L]a probabilidad guarda relación con la 'posibilidad,' pero no son equivalentes. Coinciden en el valor general de la ausencia de certeza, pero se diferencian en su presentación. [...] Un ejemplo puede ilustrar la diferencia entre ambas nociones: si preguntamos por Antonio y nuestro interlocutor no sabe dónde se encuentra en ese momento, podrá responder:
8. Quizás esté en la biblioteca.
En este caso lo que nos está diciendo es que Antonio, o bien está en la biblioteca, o bien no está allí, siendo la biblioteca el posible lugar donde dar con él. Pero cabe igualmente la otra alternativa de que esté en otra parte. En este sentido (8) equivale (es sustituible por) (9):
9. Es posible que Antonio esté en la biblioteca, la cual implica, a su vez:
10. Es posible que Antonio no esté en la biblioteca. Ahora bien, si el hablante no solo admite la posibilidad, sino que tiene fundadas razones para pensar que Antonio está efectivamente en la biblioteca –aunque no pueda asegurarlo con certeza–, entonces podrá responder:
11. Estará en la biblioteca."

2.1 SCALE OF POTENTIALITY

Regarding adverbs that express dubitative modality (a term roughly corresponding to MMP), Kovacci (1992: 60) mentions: "a semantic scale that graduates the doubt or supposition from the approximate certainty to approximate negation."[18] Further on, the author states that:

> [T]hese grades are marked also by the verbal mood: *seguramente* [(*likely*)], of positive polarity, combines with indicative; *difícilmente* [(*with difficulty*)], of negative polarity, rules the subjunctive or "unreal" tenses of the indicative (future tenses) and equals to *probablemente no* [(*probably not*)]; the remaining adverbs accept both indicative and subjunctive, graduating, thus, the expression towards one of the poles of the scale (Kovacci 1992: 160).[19]

A similar scale is proposed also by Haverkate (2002: 58):

> The defining characteristic of cognition predicates is the expression of the attitude the subject of the matrix clause adopts with respect to the truth value of the embedded proposition. [...] [T]he class of cognition predicates can be properly divided into an epistemic, a doxastic, and a dubitative subclass. The lexical properties of these subclasses can be described in terms of scalar magnitudes representing different degrees of commitment to truth value.

From the semantic point of view, an analysis of the gradation of potentiality (epistemic modality) is presented also by Kratzer (1991: 643–645).

Following this line of investigation, we also understand the relationship between potentiality and reality as a gradual relationship that can be captured on an axis. In this chapter, we will present a methodology that determines with sufficient precision the position of concrete utterances with the MMR or the MMP on this axis.

2.2 CRITERIA TO FIND THE POSITION OF AN UTTERANCE ON THE AXIS

The expression of potentiality in Spanish can have two stages: the selection of a concrete lexical expression of potentiality (LP) and the subsequent choice of mood which can either strengthen the potentiality or weaken it. This gradual expression of uncertainty is possible in those situations where the speaker is also the subject of the sen-

---

18 Original quotation (the translation is ours): "una escala semántica que gradúa la duda o la conjetura desde la aproximación a la certeza hasta la aproximación a la negación."
19 Original quotation (the translation is ours): "[E]stos grados están marcados también por el modo verbal: *seguramente*, de polaridad positiva, se construye con indicativo; *difícilmente*, de polaridad negativa, rige subjuntivo o bien tiempos 'irreales' del indicativo (los futuros) y equivale a *probablemente no*; los demás adverbios aceptan indicativo y subjuntivo, graduando así la expresión hacia un polo o el otro de la escala."

tence, i.e. after verbs in first person like *supongo* (*I suppose*) or in utterances containing an adverbial expression of potentiality like *tal vez* (*maybe*), *quizás* (*maybe, perhaps*) and in constructions with non-personal expressions such as *parece que* (*it seems that*).

To determine the position of a concrete utterance on the scale, we must imagine its centre, i.e. a moment when the speaker's attitude towards the veracity of his proposition is neutral and he presents it neither as real, neither as potential. It is practically impossible to imagine an utterance which would express zero reality and zero potentiality, however, for our purpose we understand it as an ideal construct and we mark it with 0. This way, the original scale changes into an axis:

Potentiality (P) / –Reality (R)

Image 2: Axis

In Spanish, there are two possible ways of moving on the axis between the MMR and the MMP. The first one is the selection of a concrete expression of potentiality, more precisely the force of the seme of potentiality this expression contains, we will mark this factor as *p*. The second one is the selection of verbal mood that will follow it (i.e. the alternation between the indicative and the subjunctive), we will mark this factor as *m*.

Nevertheless, the possibility of this choice is not automatic, for it is not permitted by lexical expressions of reality (LR) and even by some LPs. This leads to the conclusion that while the mood selection is important in these cases, it is also secondary regarding the choice of L.

The final potentiality of an utterance (*P*) and its final position on the axis is given by the sum of *p* and *m*. We may, therefore, state that $P = p + m$.

We understand potentiality as a mirror reflection of reality. When the speaker weakens the seme of reality, he simultaneously strengthens the seme of potentiality and the other way around. The analysis can, therefore, be taken not only from the point of view of potentiality, but also from the point of view of reality. If we mark the reality of an utterance as *R*, then we may also claim that $P = -R$ and $R = -P$.

2.2.1 DETERMINATION OF *R* – THE SELECTION OF LEXICAL EXPRESSION OF REALITY

An utterance can acquire the MM real in two situations. It can either contain a lexical expression of reality, e.g. *estoy seguro* (*I am sure*), *estoy convencido* (*I am convinced*), or it can lack any LR or LP, e.g. *José está cansado* (*José is tired*).

The category of reality / potentiality is not optional in an utterance. When we formulate an utterance, the listener expects that its content, unless stated otherwise, corresponds with reality according to the speaker. The potentiality (unlike the reality), as the marked member of this opposition, must be always expressed in an utterance, either by lexical or morphological means (or by their combination). Reality must be explicitly expressed only in those cases when the speaker needs to strengthen it. The R of those utterances that contain a lexical expression of the MM real is, thus, higher than with those that do not. If the LR is missing, R will be in the interval (0;1>, e.g. *José vendrá* (*José will come*); the interval (1;2> belongs to utterances with LR, e.g. *estoy convencido de que vendrá* (*I am convinced that he will come*); the interval (2;3> belongs to utterances with multiple strengthening of the MMR, e.g. *estoy completamente convencido de que vendrá* (*I am absolutely convinced that will come*).

2.2.2 DETERMINATION OF p – THE SELECTION OF LEXICAL EXPRESSION OF POTENTIALITY

Those lexical expressions that limit to a certain extent the validity of an utterance must contain a seme of potentiality. This seme is, nevertheless, not equally strong with all of them and speakers can choose from a whole scale of partially synonymous expression the one that reflects most accurately their commitment to the veracity of their utterance. The level of potentiality expressed by a speaker is, therefore, specified in confrontation with other LPs.

The grade of potentiality that contains a concrete LP is, at the same time, directly connected to the subsequent mood selection. There are expressions of potentiality which require the use of the subjunctive almost always (*dudo que: I doubt that*), expressions that permit both the subjunctive or the indicative (*quizás: maybe*), expressions that allow the use of the subjunctive only very seldom (*parece que: it seem that*) and, finally, those that belong to the group of LPs, but they impede the use of the subjunctive (*pienso que: I think that*).

The possibilities of mood selection are, therefore, limited to a certain level by the choice of a concrete LP. On the other hand, it is not possible to say that by choosing an LP which excludes the possibility of using the subjunctive, the speaker would abandon the sphere of potentiality and his utterance would gain the MM real. We can see that the contradiction resulting from an utterance such as *I think that he is tired, but maybe it just seems so* is much lower than in *He is tired, but maybe it just seems so*. For some speakers, the former sentence might seem appropriate, some might find it more difficult to imagine a proper context for its usage, there can be, nevertheless, no doubt that expressions such as *I think* do limit the speaker's commitment to the veracity of his utterance. We must, therefore, consider such expressions as LPs despite the fact that without the support of negation they impede the use of the subjunctive.

Nevertheless, the subjunctive is also a congruential mood and the frequency of its use should be directly related to the level of potentiality that contains an LP, since in utterances with the MMP the subjunctive congrues precisely with the seme of potentiality. The stronger this seme is, the higher is the frequency of use of the subjunctive in the dictum and the other way around: LPs with a weaker seme of potentiality loosen the congruence or impede it completely.

This leads to the conclusion that different lexical expressions of MMP must have a different value of p and, at the same time, that this value must be higher for those that prefer the use of the congruential subjunctive and lower for such LPs that enable its usage only sporadically or impede it completely.

The determination of the value of p is, therefore, possible through an analysis of concrete expressions of potentiality both from the practical and theoretical point of view. This analysis will show whether there is at least a theoretical possibility for using the subjunctive and it will compare the frequency of use of this mood with other LPs.

The initial typology consists, analogically to the expressions of reality, of three degrees. LPs that do not permit the use of the subjunctive can be considered expressions with low level of potentiality and they belong to the interval (0;1>. We expect a higher value of p (1;3> for those LPs that enable the use of the subjunctive in the dictum. Those that, nevertheless, prefer the indicative have a lower p than those that prefer the subjunctive. The former group is assigned with the interval (1;2>, the latter one with (2;3>.

2.2.3 DETERMINATION OF m – MOOD SELECTION AFTER A LEXICAL EXPRESSION OF MMP

The choice of mood is the second instrument for graduating potentiality in Spanish. However, strengthening or lowering of the seme of potentiality of a concrete lexical expression is possible only in those situations where the speaker uses a verbal mood that can be considered as marked in the given context.

Especially non-native speakers (but not only them) tend to presuppose that given the choice between the indicative and the subjunctive, the former one is always the unmarked member while the subjunctive adds a certain special value to an utterance. We propose that the subjunctive can be considered as the marked member of the opposition only in those cases where its use is not common.

As we have already stated, the use of the subjunctive is very frequent with those LPs that contain a high level of potentiality ($p > 2$) and the use of the indicative is sporadic in such cases. The same can be stated for the opposite situation: LPs with $p < 2$ give more space for the use of the indicative. There are, therefore, both utterances where the marked mood is the subjunctive and those where the marked mood is the indicative. RAE (2009: 1910), for example, points out that after expressions such as *no creo* (*I do not believe*) o *no me parece* (*it doesn't seem to me*) the indicative is used very seldom for its use would suggest a logical contradiction between the contents of the main and the dependent clause (i.e. denying something that is subsequently presented as real via the indicative). It would be, therefore, incorrect to suppose that in these cases the function of the subjunctive is to strengthen potentiality.

Opposite rule applies for LPs that have their p in the interval (1;2>; it is the indicative that prevails with them as clearly states Sastre Ruano (1997: 81):

[P]recisely given the moderate affirmation they suggest, constructions with V_1 such as *creer* [(*to believe*)], *sospechar* [(*to suspect*)] etc. would be less frequent. For some speakers, but not for everyone, the following sequences would be unacceptable:

Sospecho que mi hija haya querido coger el coche y no haya podido sacarlo del garaje.

[(*I suspect that my daughter wanted-subj. to take the car and she could-subj. not take it out from the garage.*)]

Admito que lo hayas pagado tú, pero no puedo aceptarlo.

[(*I admit that you have-subj. payed, but I cannot accept it.*)]

Creo que salga pronto, pero vete tú a saber.

[(*I believe he will get-subj. out soon, but who knows.*)]

It must be especially stated that all these constructions are only acceptable in very limited and specific communication contexts.[20]

The value of m must be, therefore, always determined with regard to p, for they are closely linked. Its determination makes no sense in those cases where p is lower than one, since the modal alternation is not possible, m is, thus, relevant only when $p > 1$. Its value can be 0 if the speaker uses the unmarked mood. It can be 1 if the subjunctive is used after an expression with p in the interval (1;2> and we can suppose that this mood strengthens its potentiality. Finally, its value can be –1 if the speaker decides for an LP with p higher than 2 but, with the indicative, he immediately weakens this seme.

We can summarize the previous observations in this way:

1) $p \leq 1$ – The alternation between the subjunctive and the indicative is not possible and m is not relevant (or we can state that it equals 0).

$p \leq 1 \rightarrow m = 0$

2) $p > 1 \wedge p \leq 2$ – Using the subjunctive, the speaker can strengthen the potentiality of his utterance, and m equals 1. The indicative is the unmarked member in these situations, its use means that m equals 0.

$p > 1 \wedge p \leq 2$ + indicative $\rightarrow m = 0$

$p > 1 \wedge p \leq 2$ + subjunctive $\rightarrow m = 1$

3) $p > 2$ – This case is opposite to the previous one. The subjunctive is used commonly after expressions with such a high level of potentiality and its use does not increase the value of P, therefore $m = 0$. However, the level of potentiality can be reduced by the indicative that is used less frequently after these LPs. In those cases, m equals –1.

$p > 2$ + subjunctive $\rightarrow m = 0$

$p > 2$ + indicative $\rightarrow m = -1$

---

20 Original quotation (the translation is ours): "[P]recisamente por lo que suponen de afirmación atenuada, serían mucho menos frecuentes las construcciones cuyos V_1 son *creer, admitir, sospechar*, etc. hasta el punto de que para algunos hablantes –que no para todos– serían inaceptables las secuencias siguientes:

Sospecho que mi hija haya querido coger el coche y no haya podido sacarlo del garaje.

Admito que lo hayas pagado tú, pero no puedo aceptarlo.

Creo que salga pronto, pero vete tú a saber.

Hay que señalar de forma especial que todas estas construcciones solamente son aceptables en unos contextos comunicativos muy restringidos y específicos."

2.3 DETERMINATION OF p – ANALYSIS OF CONCRETE LPS

We shall now proceed to determine the values of p of concrete expressions of potentiality. At first, we divide them into two groups:

1) Adverbs expressing potentiality: *quizá(s)* (*maybe, perhaps*), *tal vez* (*maybe*), *probablemente* (*probably*), *posiblemente* (*possibly*), *seguramente* (*likely*), *acaso* (*perhaps*), *a lo mejor* (*maybe*) and non-personal expressions: *parece que* (*it seemes that*), *puede ser que* (*it can be that*), *es posible* (*it is possible*), *es probable* (*it is probable*).

2) Verbs expressing potentiality: *creer* (*to believe*), *pensar* (*to think*), *dudar* (*to doubt*), *no saber* (*to not know*).

2.3.1 ADVERBS EXPRESSING POTENTIALITY AND NON-PERSONAL EXPRESSIONS *PARECE QUE, PUEDE SER QUE, ES POSIBLE QUE, ES PROBABLE QUE*

Spanish has several adverbs that can be followed either by the indicative or by the subjunctive: *quizá(s)* (*maybe, perhaps*), *tal vez* (*maybe*), *probablemente* (*probably*), *posiblemente* (*possibly*), *seguramente* (*likely*), *acaso* (*perhaps*). The list can be completed by the adverb *a lo mejor* that also means *maybe* or *perhaps*. Traditionally, grammars have considered incorrect the use of the subjunctive after this adverb, however, it has been recently admitted as a valid option by the normative grammar by RAE (2009: 1956–1957).

Grammars generally state that the choice of mood depends on the level of speaker's commitment to the veracity of his proposition. Sastre Ruano (1997: 48) proposes the following explanation:

> [*Tal vez, quizá(s), posiblemente, seguramente, acaso, probablemente*] [c]an be construed with the indicative or the subjunctive. Generally, when there is a major grade of probability of the fulfillment, the indicative appears; when speaking about less probable actions, it is the subjunctive that appears. [...] Nevertheless, in practice, the context, the situation and communicative intentions of the speaker are the keys to decide whether to use forms of one or the other mood, together with the wish whether to accentuate or not the speaker's doubt. It is the speaker who chooses the grade of certainty he wants to give to his message, the use of one of the two moods does not depend exactly on the real grade of probability, but on the impression the speaker has or wishes to give.[21]

21　Original quotation (the translation is ours): "[*Tal vez, quizá(s), posiblemente, seguramente, acaso, probablemente*] [p]ueden construirse con indicativo o subjuntivo. En general, cuando existe un mayor grado de probabilidad de que se cumpla aparece el indicativo; y cuando se trata de acciones menos probables es el subjuntivo que aparece. [...] Pero en la práctica son el contexto, la situación y las intenciones comunicativas del hablante las claves que deciden la utilización de formas de uno u otro modo, además, de un deseo de acentuar o no más la duda por parte del emisor. Es el hablante el que elige el grado de seguridad que le quiere dar a su mensaje, y por eso la utilización de uno u otro modo no depende exactamente del grado de probabilidad real, sino de la impresión que el hablante tenga o quiera dar."

Similar rules apply with the choice of mood after *parece que* (*it seems that*). Ridruejo (1999: 3223) claims that "[t]his verb admits the alternation of both moods, indicative and subjunctive, in the subordinate clause, when construed as non-pronominal, i.e. meaning 'semejar' [(to look like)], 'resultar una determinada apariencia' [(to produce certain appearance)]."[22] We study this construction together with adverbs expressing potentiality because their functions are basically the same. We agree with Nowikow (2001: 88) who observes that "this verb modalizes the content in a way similar to dubitative adverbs like *quizá, tal vez, acaso* or *probablemente, posiblemente* etc."[23] We approach in the same way another non-personal expression *puede* (*ser*) *que* (*it can be that*).

Based on the observations from Spanish grammars, these LPs should belong into the interval (1;3>). We will analyse concrete frequencies of the use of the subjunctive and the indicative in the following corpus analysis.

2.3.1.1 CORPUS ANALYSIS

2.3.1.1.1 QUIZÁ(S), TAL VEZ, PROBABLEMENTE, POSIBLEMENTE, ACASO, SEGURAMENTE, A LO MEJOR, PARECE QUE, PUEDE SER QUE

The following analyses were conducted in March 2017 in the subcorpus containing only Spanish originals (11 962 165 tokens). That was further divided into two parts: Spanish authors (3 971 374, i.e. 33% of the original subcorpus) and Latin American authors (7 990 788, i.e. 67% of the original subcorpus). When analysing the data, it is therefore important to bear in mind that the Spanish part is considerably smaller than the Latin American one.

The analysis concentrates also on the idiolect of concrete authors and is limited to literary texts. For an analysis of Spanish adverbs of potentiality conducted on the larger corpus CREA (with no reference to the uses by concrete authors), refer to Aurová (2013; an exhaustive analysis of the adverb *quizá(s)*), Barrios Sabador (2015, 2016; special reference to spoken language) and Kratochvílová (2013a; a contrastive analysis Spanish-Czech, conducted on CREA and InterCorp).

All the queries had an analogical form:

[word="[pP]robablemente"],

the only exceptions being *tal vez* and *parece que* where we used a lemma:

22 Original quotation (the translation is ours): "[e]ste verbo admite en la oración subordinada en función de atributo la alternancia de ambos modos, indicativo y subjuntivo, en construcción no pronominal, esto es, con el significado 'semejar', 'resultar una determinada apariencia'."
23 Original quotation (the translation is ours): "este verbo modaliza el contenido de forma parecida a la de como lo hacen los adverbios dubitativos del tipo *quizá, tal vez, acaso o probablemente, posiblemente*, etc."

[lemma="tal~vez"],
[!word="[mM]e | [tT]e | [lL]e | [nN]os | [oO]s | [lL]es | [sS]e | [nN]o"]
[lemma="parecer"][word="que"]

and *puede (ser) que* with the following form of query:

[!word="[nN]o"][word="[pP]uede"][word="ser"]?[word="que"].

Further on, all the concordances were controlled manually in order to eliminate any results that were not relevant for our study or that might distort the analysis. Our criteria for processing the results were as follows:

1) We always analysed all uses of a concrete LP and indicated the frequency of use of the indicative and the subjunctive. We did not indicate the uses of the conditional.
2) We analysed only those cases where the LPs appeared in front of the verb and were not separated by commas.
3) We excluded all constructions where the choice of mood could have been influenced by factors other than the presence of an LP (e.g. concessive clauses, conditional clauses).
4) From the results were also excluded frequent constructions of the following type: *quizás por eso* + VERB (*maybe because of it* + VERB), *quizás es que* + VERB (*maybe it is that* + VERB) etc.
5) The *hablaré* paradigm is considered indicative here. Given the limited context we had and the fact that both the probabilitive and the indicative are non-congruential moods, we do not distinguish here between them.
6) The *hubiera(-se) hablado* paradigms were also excluded from the data, for they often substitute the past conditional (i.e. a non-congruential mood) which could also distort the results.[24]
7) When analysing the adverb *acaso*, we excluded all its uses with the conjunction *si* (*if*)[25] and its appearances in interrogative sentences.[26]
8) With *parece que*, we only considered its uses as impersonal construction that is not negated, we excluded all its uses with reflexive pronouns (*me parece que*: *it seems to me that*).
9) Finally, the data do not reflect those situations where the LP was not followed by a verb, such as *puede que sí* (*maybe yes*).

---

24   This paradigm originally expresses the pluperfect subjunctive; however, it is often used to substitute the past conditional *habría hablado*.
25   The construction *por si acaso* is a lexicalized expression meaning *just in case*.
26   In Spanish, *acaso* is often used in rhetorical questions such as *¿Acaso no te lo he dicho mil veces?* (*Haven't I told you this a thousand times?*) where it does not function as a proper dubitative adverb.

Table 4: *Choice of mood after* quizá(s)

QUIZÁ(S)	Indicative	Subjunctive	% IND / SUBJ
SPAIN			
Cela	—	17	0 / 100
Cercas	28	4	87.5 / 12.5
Cunqueiro	1	2	
Delibes	—	1	
Etxebarría	46	43	51.7 / 48.3
Laforet	5	5	
Llamazares	11	10	52.4 / 47.6
Marías	262	72	78.4 / 21.6
Marsé	16	4	80 / 20
Martín Santos	3	1	
Mendoza	3	1	
Moro	26	34	43.3 / 56.7
Navarro	9	3	
Ortega y Gasset	—	1	
Pérez-Reverte	96	111	46.4 / 53.6
Sanmartín Fenollera	6	9	40 / 60
Sierra	11	22	33.3 / 66.7
Silva	—	6	
Torres	6	2	
Tusset	16	18	47.1 / 52.9
Vila Matas	3	6	
Total for the area	**548**	**372**	**59.6 / 40.4**
LATIN AMERICA			
Allende	1	1	
Andahazi	—	6	
Arenas	1	1	
Benedetti	24	52	31.6 / 68.4
Bioy Casares	5	19	20.8 / 79.2
Bolaño	2	—	
Borges	8	3	

Bucay, Salinas	11	22	33.3 / 66.7
Cortázar	45	34	57 / 43
Fuentes	44	14	75.9 / 24.1
García Márquez	24	12	66.7 / 33.3
Gutiérrez	9	—	
Chaviano	4	12	25 / 75
Montero	3	3	
Roa Bastos	2	2	
Rulfo	9	14	39.1 / 60.9
Sabato	23	15	60.5 / 39.5
Valdés	—	1	
Vargas Llosa	15	36	29.4 / 70.6
Zúñiga Pavlov	31	17	64.6 / 35.4
Total for the area	**261**	**264**	**49.7 / 50.3**
Total	**809**	**636**	**56 / 44**

Weighted average (authors who had at least 15 relevant uses of *quizá(s)* + IND / SUBJ)
INDICATIVE 1064 : 22 = 48.4%
SUBJUNCTIVE 1136 : 22 = 51.6%

Table 5: Choice of mood after tal vez

TAL VEZ	Indicative	Subjunctive	% IND / SUBJ
	SPAIN		
Almodóvar	1	8	
Bécquer	1	—	
Cela	—	3	
Cercas	5	1	
Delibes	4	1	
Etxebarría	2	—	
Laforet	13	—	
Llamazares	1	—	
Marías	101	21	82.8 / 17.2
Marsé	13	1	

Martín Santos	5	11	31.3 / 68.7
Mendoza	14	14	50 / 50
Moro	1	—	
Navarro	—	1	
Ortega y Gasset	4	7	
Pérez-Reverte	164	118	58.2 / 41.8
Sanmartín Fenollera	9	7	56.2 / 43.8
Sierra	13	25	34.2 / 65.8
Silva	1	—	
Torres	2	—	
Unamuno	5	—	
Vila Matas	7	7	
Total for the area	**366**	**225**	**61.9 / 38.1**
LATIN AMERICA			
Allende	181	91	66.5 / 33.5
Andahazi	—	4	
Arenas	4	6	
Benedetti	6	34	15 / 85
Bioy Casares	13	51	20.3 / 79.7
Bolaño	109	81	57.4 / 42.6
Borges	108	39	73.5 / 26.5
Bucay, Salinas	4	6	
Carpentier	2	9	
Cortázar	28	24	53.8 / 46.2
García Márquez	65	40	61.9 / 38.1
Gutiérrez	3	—	
Chaviano	3	7	
Montero	11	5	68.8 / 31.2
Quiroga	—	3	
Roa Bastos	15	5	75 / 25
Rulfo	15	15	50 / 50
Sabato	15	12	55.6 / 44.4
Sacheri	14	17	45.2 / 54.8
Sepúlveda	1	1	

Valdés	5	3	
Vargas Llosa	103	47	68.7 / 31.3
Zúñiga Pavlov	1	2	
Total for the area	**706**	**502**	**58.4 / 41.6**
Total	**1072**	**727**	**59.6 / 40.4**

Weighted average (authors who had at least 15 relevant uses of *tal vez* + IND / SUBJ)

INDICATIVE 1024.4 : 19 = 53.9%
SUBJUNCTIVE 875.6 : 19 = 46.1%

Table 6: Choice of mood after probablemente

PROBABLEMENTE	Indicative	Subjunctive	% IND / SUBJ
SPAIN			
Almodóvar	1	4	
Cela	3	—	
Etxebarría	9	6	60 / 40
Laforet	1	—	
Marías	12	—	
Marsé	4	—	
Martín Santos	1	—	
Mendoza	4	—	
Moro	1	1	
Navarro	1	—	
Ortega y Gasset	1	—	
Pérez-Reverte	1	—	
Sierra	5	—	
Sanmartín Fenollera	9	2	
Unamuno	1	—	
Vila Matas	2	1	
Total for the area	**56**	**14**	**80 / 20**
LATIN AMERICA			
Allende	13	—	
Arriaga	—	1	
Benedetti	6	2	

Bolaño	110	17	86.6 / 13.4
Bucay, Salinas	—	4	
Cortázar	35	1	97.2 / 2.8
Fuentes	2	—	
García Márquez	3	—	
Roa Bastos	1	—	
Sabato	2	—	
Sacheri	—	4	
Valdés	—	1	
Vargas Llosa	19	1	95 / 5
Zúñiga Pavlov	3	—	
Total for the area	**194**	**31**	**86.2 / 13.8**
Total	**250**	**45**	**84.7 / 15.3**

Weighted average (authors who had at least 15 relevant uses of *probablemente* + IND / SUBJ)

INDICATIVE 338.8 : 4 = 84.7

SUBJUNCTIVE 61.2 : 4 = 15.3

Table 7: Choice of mood after posiblemente

POSIBLEMENTE	Indicative	Subjunctive	% IND / SUBJ
SPAIN			
Marías	3	1	
Marsé	1	—	
Mendoza	—	1	
Moro	—	1	
Pérez-Reverte	3	2	
Silva	—	1	
Tusset	—	1	
Vila Matas	1	—	
Total for the area	**8**	**7**	**53.3 / 46.7**
LATIN AMERICA			
Allende	33	16	67.3 / 32.7
Bioy Casares	1	—	
Bolaño	17	3	85 / 15

	Indicative	Subjunctive	% IND / SUBJ
Borges	1	—	
Bucay, Salinas	—	2	
García Márquez	1	—	
Chaviano	—	1	
Montero	1	—	
Quiroga	1	—	
Sepúlveda	1	—	
Total for the area	**56**	**22**	**71.8 / 28.2**
Total	**64**	**29**	**68.8 / 31.2**

Weighted average (authors who had at least 15 relevant uses of *posiblemente* + IND / SUBJ)

INDICATIVE 152.3 : 2 = 76.2%
SUBJUNCTIVE 47.7 : 2 = 23.8%

Table 8: Choice of mood after acaso

ACASO	Indicative	Subjunctive	% IND / SUBJ
SPAIN			
Bécquer	9	11	45 / 55
Cela	7	—	
Etxebarría	5	—	
Laforet	22	3	88 / 12
Marías	3	1	
Mendoza	8	1	
Moro	2	1	
Navarro	2	17	10.5 / 89.5
Ortega y Gasset	1	—	
Sierra	2	2	
Tusset	16	15	51.6 / 48.4
Unamuno	3	4	
Vila Matas	1	—	
Total for the area	**81**	**55**	**59.6 / 40.4**
LATIN AMERICA			
Allende	2	—	
Andahazi	1	—	

Arriaga	2	—	
Bioy Casares	2	2	
Bolaño	23	7	76.7 / 23.3
Borges	15	16	48.4 / 51.6
Bucay, Salinas	1	1	
Carpentier	8	6	
Coloane	13	—	
Fuentes	6	3	
Montero	—	1	
Onetti	8	4	
Quiroga	—	2	
Roa Bastos	5	3	
Rulfo	6	5	
Valdés	22	5	81.5 / 18.5
Vargas Llosa	5	—	
Total for the area	**119**	**55**	**68.4 / 31.6**
Total	**200**	**110**	**64.5 / 35.5**

Weighted average (authors who had at least 15 relevant *uses of acaso* + IND / SUBJ)

INDICATIVE 401.7 : 7 = 57.5%
SUBJUNCTIVE 298.3 : 7 = 42.5%

Table 9: Choice of mood after seguramente

SEGURAMENTE	Indicative	Subjunctive	% IND / SUBJ
SPAIN			
Almodóvar	1	—	
Cela	8	—	
Etxebarría	1	—	
Laforet	3	—	
Llamazares	3	—	
Marías	40	—	100 / 0
Marsé	20	—	
Martín Santos	2		

Mendoza	4	—	
Moro	8	—	
Navarro	12	—	
Pérez-Reverte	6	—	
Sanmartín Fenollera	14	—	
Sierra	2	—	
Silva	6	—	
Vila Matas	2	—	
Total for the area	**132**	**0**	**100 / 0**
LATIN AMERICA			
Allende	57	—	100 / 0
Arenas	6	—	
Benedetti	25	—	100 / 0
Bolaño	70	—	100 / 0
Bucay, Salinas	7	1	
Carpentier	1	—	
Coloane	3	—	
Cortázar	9	—	
Fuentes	1	—	
Gutiérrez	2	—	
Chaviano	4	—	
Montero	11	—	
Quiroga	1	—	
Roa Bastos	1	—	
Rulfo	6	—	
Sabato	25	—	100 / 0
Sacheri	1	—	
Sepúlveda	1	—	
Vargas Llosa	23	—	100 / 0
Zúñiga Pavlov	3	—	
Total for the area	**257**	**1**	**99.6 / 0.4**
Total	**389**	**1**	**99.7 / 0.3**

Table 10: Choice of mood after a lo mejor

A LO MEJOR	Indicative	Subjunctive	% IND / SUBJ
Almodóvar	1	—	
Cela	24	—	100 / 0
Cercas	7	—	
Cunqueiro	5	—	
Delibes	10	—	
Etxebarría	1	—	
Jiménez Lozano	19	—	100 / 0
Marías	21	—	100 / 0
Marsé	7	—	
Martín Santos	3	—	
Mendoza	5	—	
Moro	2	—	
Navarro	24	—	100 / 0
Pérez-Reverte	26	—	100 / 0
Sierra	1	—	
Silva	7	—	
Torres	5	—	
Tusset	1	—	
Total for the area	**169**	**0**	**100 / 0**
Arenas	1	—	
Benedetti	27	—	100 / 0
Bioy Casares	1	—	
Borges	3	—	
Bucay, Salinas	5	—	
Coloane	1	—	
Cortázar	127	—	100 / 0
García Márquez	2	—	
Gutiérrez	6	—	
Chaviano	22	—	100 / 0
Montero	18	—	100 / 0
Onetti	3	—	

Roa Bastos	1	—	
Rulfo	1	—	
Sabato	6	—	
Sacheri	2	—	
Sepúlveda	4	—	
Valdés	6	—	
Vargas Llosa	93	—	100 / 0
Zúñiga Pavlov	1	—	
Total for the area	**330**	**0**	**100 / 0**
Total	**499**	**0**	**100 / 0**

Table 11: Choice of mood after parece que

PARECE QUE	Indicative	Subjunctive	% IND / SUBJ
	SPAIN		
Almodóvar	3	1	
Bécquer	8	—	
Cela	23	—	100 / 0
Cunqueiro	4	5	
Delibes	26	4	86.7 / 13.3
Etxebarría	18	5	78.3 / 21.7
Laforet	16	3	84.2 / 15.8
Marías	12	11	
Marsé	25	4	86.2 / 13.8
Martín Santos	12	—	
Mendoza	5	—	
Moro	29	9	76.3 / 23.7
Navarro	12	1	
Ortega y Gasset	2	—	
Pérez-Reverte	19	32	37.3 / 62.7
Sanmartín Fenollera	6	—	
Sierra	10	—	
Silva	1	—	
Torres	2	3	

Tusset	7	4	
Unamuno	14	—	
Vila Matas	1	1	
Total for the area	**255**	**83**	**75.4 / 24.6**
LATIN AMERICA			
Allende	35	1	97.2 / 2.8
Arenas	7	1	
Arriaga	3	—	
Benedetti	22	2	91.7 / 8.3
Bioy Casares	4	1	
Bolaño	29	4	87.9 / 12.1
Borges	3	—	
Bucay, Salinas	6	—	
Carpentier	18	13	58.1 / 41.9
Coloane	6	3	
Cortázar	54	2	96.4 / 3.6
Fuentes	8	1	
García Márquez	13	6	68.4 / 31.6
Gutiérrez	3	—	
Chaviano	1	—	
Montero	3	—	
Onetti	9	—	
Quiroga	—	1	
Roa Bastos	6	—	
Rulfo	14	2	87.5 / 12.5
Sabato	10	2	
Sacheri	14	—	
Sepúlveda	7	1	
Valdés	6	—	
Vargas Llosa	86	24	78.2 / 21.8
Zúñiga Pavlov	7	5	58.3 / 41.7
Total for the area	**374**	**69**	**84.4 / 15.6**
Total	**629**	**152**	**80.5 / 19.5**

Weighted average (authors who had at least 15 relevant uses of *parece que* + IND / SUBJ)
INDICATIVE 1272.7 : 16 = 79.5%
SUBJUNCTIVE 327.3 : 16 = 20.5%

Table 12: Choice of mood after puede (ser) que

PUEDE (SER) QUE	Indicative	Subjunctive	% IND / SUBJ
Cela	—	4	
Delibes	—	2	
Etxebarría	—	24	0 / 100
Marías	—	66	0 / 100
Marsé	—	4	
Moro	—	2	
Navarro	—	22	0 / 100
Pérez-Reverte	—	34	0 / 100
Sanmartín Fenollera	—	1	
Sierra	—	3	
Silva	—	2	
Torres	—	6	
Tusset	—	18	0 / 100
Unamuno	—	1	
Total for the area	**0**	**189**	**0 / 100**
Allende	—	8	
Benedetti	—	6	
Bolaño	—	124	0 / 100
Bucay, Salinas	—	1	
Cortázar	—	11	
Fuentes	—	15	0 / 100
García Márquez	—	9	
Gutiérrez	—	1	
Chaviano	—	2	
Onetti	—	4	
Roa Bastos	—	5	

Rulfo	—	2	
Sabato	—	2	
Sepúlveda	—	2	
Valdés	—	2	
Vargas Llosa	—	27	0 / 100
Total for the area	**0**	**221**	**0 / 100**
Total	**0**	**410**	**0 / 100**

Based on the analysis, we can conclude that the choice of mood does not seem to be influenced by the nationality of the author. The only major discordance can be found with *posiblemente* (the indicative was used in 53.3% of cases in books by Spanish authors and in 71.8% in books by Latin American authors), nevertheless, the total amount of data on which we base the analysis is relatively small in this case (only 93 appearances in total).

On the other hand, the choice of mood (and the choice of a concrete LP as well) does prove to be influenced by the idiolect of a concrete author in some cases. When analysing the most frequent pair *quizá(s)* and *tal vez*, we rarely find an author that would use them with the same frequency (the only possible exceptions being Javier Sierra, Juan Marsé and Natalia Sanmartín Fenollera). Generally, there is a great difference in the frequency the authors use one of these two adverbs. The disproportion is striking for example with the Chilean authors Isabel Allende (only 2 uses of *quizá(s)* and 272 uses of *tal vez*) and Jorge Zúñiga Pavlov (47 uses of *quizá(s)* and only 3 uses of *tal vez*) or with the Spanish authors Javier Marías (334 uses of *quizá(s)* and 122 uses of *tal vez*) and Arturo Pérez-Reverte (207 uses of *quizá(s)* and 282 uses of *tal vez*).

The influence of author's idiolect on the choice of mood can be observed for example with the Spanish authors Javier Marías (the indicative after *quizá(s)* was used in 78.4% of cases) and Pérez-Reverte (the indicative appeared only with the frequency of 46.4% after the same adverb). A major discordance can also be found with the adverb *tal vez*. In books by Jorge Luis Borges, this adverb was followed by the indicative in 73.5% of cases, yet in the books by another Argentinian author, Adolfo Bioy Casares, the frequency of the indicative was only 20.3%.

The preference for a concrete mood after a concrete adverb can sometimes be observed even within the idiolect of one single author. Mario Benedetti (Latin America – Uruguay) uses the indicative after *quizá(s)* in 31.6% of cases, but with *tal vez* the same mood appears only in 15% of cases. An opposite tendency can be observed in the texts by Mario Vargas Llosa (Latin America – Peru) who uses the indicative after *quizá(s)* with the frequency of 29.4%, after *tal vez* the indicative appears in 68.7% of cases.

This confirms the above presented theory that the choice of mood is secondary with respect to the selection of a concrete modalizer. The level of potentiality is not the same in different LPs and it is precisely this level of potentiality that (dis)favours the use of the subjunctive. However, even the level of potentiality of one single LP need not to be perceived in the same way by different speakers (this being the only possible explanation for major discrepancies in the choice of mood among different authors). The above presented axis can, therefore, be understood not only as a generalizing instrument that helps us to determine the level of potentiality of a concrete LP, it could also be used to represent the perception of the MMP inside an idiolect of a concrete speaker. Such axes would differ slightly in the same way the preference for the subjunctive or the indicative after an LP differs among concrete speakers.

However, the main goal of the analysis was to find out which LPs prefer the congruential mood and which are those that make its use harder, eliminating, if possible, the influence of the idiolect of those authors that have more extensive texts in the corpus. From this point of view, we consider the weighted average the most reliable indicator for the comparison of different LPs. We expressed in per cent the frequency of the use of the indicative and the subjunctive after one LP with those authors that used it at least in 15 relevant cases. Consequently, we calculated the weighted average from these results. The frequencies are resumed in Table 13.

Table 13: LPs according to the frequency of use of the subjunctive

LP	Frequency of the use of the subjunctive (according to weighted average)
Puede (ser) que	100.0%
Quizá(s)	51.6%
Tal vez	46.1%
Acaso	42.5%
Posiblemente	23.8%
Parece que	20.5%
Probablemente	15.3%
Seguramente	0.0%
A lo mejor	0.0%

The corpus data confirm that the subjunctive is used with different frequency after the analysed adverbs. The only construction which requires its use always is *puede (ser) que*, RAE does not admit the use of the indicative (2009: 1957) which was corroborated by the corpus data. The other LPs allowed the use of both moods, the subjunctive appeared most often after *quizá(s)*, *tal vez* and *acaso* (ca. in one half of their uses), while *posiblemente*, *probablemente* and *parece que* accept the congruential mood with greater difficulties (ca. in one fourth of their uses). We found no appearance of *a lo mejor* + subjunctive in our subcorpus and only one appearance of *seguramente* + subjunctive.

Such strong discrepancies in the mood selection after partially synonymous expressions confirm that the level of potentiality the subjunctive congrues with is not the same with all of them. In the axis, *puede (ser) que, quizá(s), tal vez* and *acaso* correspond to the interval (2;3>, the rest correspond to the interval (1;2>, i.e. among expressions that allow the use of the subjunctive, but its usage is rare and can be considered marked. Within the interval (1;2>, *posiblemente, parece que* and *probablemente* would be closer to 2 while *seguramente* and *a lo mejor* are closer to 1.

It might seem inappropriate to include *parece que* among the adverbs that express potentiality because the semantic consequences that result from using the subjunctive appear to be of a different sort here. Ridruejo (1999: 3224) observes that "with the indicative, the suspension of the truth of the subordinated proposition is proposed; on the contrary, the subjunctive entails not only the suspension of the asseveration, but a falsehood of the proposition."[27] However, the corpus analysis does not suggest that this kind of explanation could be applied on all the appearances of *parece que* + subjunctive. Compare the following examples:

"¿Qué te pasó en la cara? ¿Te volvió a picar una abeja?" "Sí, debe haber sido una abeja." "No sé. Por la hinchazón más bien parece que haya sido una avispa. O una de esas hormigas gigantes." "Puede ser," dije con la convicción profesional de un entomólogo.
What happened to your face? Were you bitten by a bee again?" "Yes, it must have been a bee." "I don't know, based on the swelling it rather seems that it has-subj. been a wasp. Or one of these giant ants." "Could be," I said with the professional conviction of an entomologist.
(ÚČNK – InterCorp. 30.03.2017. Mario Benedetti – *La borra del café*, the English translation is ours.)

Parecía que sonriendo ella tratara de hacerme sonreír también.
It seemed that with her smile, she tried-subj. to make me smile as well.
(ÚČNK – InterCorp. 30.03.2017. Carmen Laforet – *Nada*, the English translation is ours.)

Cristina y Rosa son las dos bastante altas, y parece que la gente las trate de otra manera, pero yo he salido bajita como mamá, y eso no es ninguna suerte.
Cristina and Rosa are both pretty tall and it seems that people treat-subj. them in a different way, but I am short like my mom, and that is no luck.
(ÚČNK – InterCorp. 30.03.2017. Lucía Etxebarría – *Amor, curiosidad, prozac y dudas*, the English translation is ours.)

Y estaba llorando, de eso no le cabía duda, pero también parecía que se estuviera riendo, llorando y riéndose al mismo tiempo. ¿Me entiende?
And that he was crying, there could be no doubt about that, but it also seemed that he was-subj. laughing, crying and laughing at the same time. Do you understand?
(ÚČNK – InterCorp. 30.03.2017. Roberto Bolaño – *2066*, the English translation is ours.)

Parece que encendiesen una luz allá arriba. Trae el rubio cabello suelto por la espalda, y una rosa blanca en la mano derecha.

---

27 Original quotation (the translation is ours): "con el indicativo, efectivamente, se propone por parte del hablante la suspensión de la verdad de la proposición subordinada; en cambio, el subjuntivo conlleva, no ya la suspensión de la aseveración, sino la falsedad de la proposición."

It seems that they turned-subj. *on the light up there. The blond one has loose hair and he brings a white rose in his right hand.*
(ÚČNK – InterCorp. 30.03.2017. Álvaro Cunqueiro – *Un hombre que se parecía a Orestes*, the English translation is ours.)

The proposition of the subordinate clause cannot be understood as untruthful in any of these examples. The use of the subjunctive does not necessarily imply a contra-factual interpretation, it merely strengthens the potentiality and accents the uncertainty of the speaker and his doubts. In the above cited examples, the subjunctive does not deny the veracity of a proposition, it stresses the non-reality (i.e. -R) and elevates the value of P.

2.3.1.1.2 SER POSIBLE QUE, SER PROBABLE QUE

Last type of constructions that will be analysed in this section are utterances with *es posible* (*it is possible*) and *es probable* (*it is probable*). Despite their apparent similarity with *posiblemente* (*possibly*) and *probablemente* (*probably*), the subjunctive is not used with the same frequency after them. While *posiblemente* and, especially, *probablemente* show a clear tendency to prefer the indicative, *es probable* and *es posible* generally select the subjunctive (the selection of the indicative would not be ungrammatical, but we have not found a single case in our corpus).

The analysis took place in the same subcorpus and in the same period as the previous ones, we used the lemma "ser" (*to be*) in order to find uses of *ser posible / probable* (*to be possible / probable*) in all tenses. The queries had the following form:

[!word="[nN]o"&!word="¿"][lemma="ser"][word="probable"][word="que"],
[!word="[nN]o"&!word="¿"][lemma="ser"][word="probable"][word="que"].

These query types excluded those cases where the construction was negated or it introduced a question (*Is it possible that...?*), we subsequently excluded manually other cases where *es posible / probable que* formed part of direct or indirect question (i.e. the utterance also contained the MM interrogative).

Table 14: Choice of mood after ser posible que

SER POSIBLE QUE	Indicative	Subjunctive	% IND / SUBJ
SPAIN			
Bécquer	—	1	
Cela	—	2	
Cercas	—	2	
Delibes	—	1	

Etxebarría	—	3	
Laforet	—	1	
Marías	—	18	0 / 100
Marsé	—	1	
Martín Santos	—	1	
Mendoza	—	8	
Moro	—	3	
Navarro	—	4	
Ortega y Gasset	—	2	
Pérez-Reverte	—	17	0 / 100
Sanmartín Fenollera	—	4	
Silva	—	3	
Torres	—	2	
Tusset	—	5	
Vila Matas	—	2	
Total for the area	**0**	**80**	**0 / 100**
LATIN AMERICA			
Allende	—	6	
Arenas	—	1	
Benedetti	—	2	
Bioy Casares	—	5	
Bolaño	—	15	
Cortázar	—	4	
García Márquez	—	10	
Onetti	—	5	
Roa Bastos	—	1	
Sabato	—	5	
Sacheri	—	2	
Sepúlveda	—	2	
Vargas Llosa	—	21	
Total for the area	**0**	**79**	**0 / 100**
Total	**0**	**159**	**0 / 100**

Table 15: Choice of mood after ser probable que

SER PROBABLE QUE	Indicative	Subjunctive	% IND / SUBJ
SPAIN			
Cercas	—	2	
Marías	—	7	
Marsé	—	2	
Mendoza	—	1	
Moro	—	1	
Pérez-Reverte	—	2	
Sanmartín Fenollera	—	1	
Sierra	—	6	
Tusset	—	3	
Total for the area	**0**	**25**	**0 / 100**
LATIN AMERICA			
Arenas	—	1	
Benedetti	—	15	0 / 100
Bolaño	—	7	
Bucay, Salinas	—	1	
Carpentier	—	6	
Cortázar	—	1	
García Márquez	—	5	
Onetti	—	2	
Roa Bastos	—	1	
Sabato	—	10	
Sacheri	—	2	
Vargas Llosa	—	2	
Total for the area	**0**	**53**	**0 / 100**
Total	**0**	**78**	**0 / 100**

Such latent discrepancy between the mood selection with *posiblemente / probablemente* and *es posible / es probable* might seem surprising. As observed by Hummel (2004: 128): "It is interesting to see that *es probable / posible* correlate preferably with the subjunctive, while *probablemente* and *posiblemente* correlate rather with the indicative, even though there cannot be observed any notable semantic difference."[28] According to the author, it is the conjunction *que* (particle in Hummel's terminology) that plays the decisive role and opens the way for using the subjunctive (see Hummel 2004: 130–131).

We suggest an alternative explanation that is based on our concept of modality. We disagree with Hummel's opinion that there is no semantic difference between the adverbs *posiblemente* and *probablemente* and the constructions *es posible / probable que*. The synonymy here is only apparent. While *posiblemente* and *probablemente* are adverbs expressing the MMP and, consequently, the level of speaker's certainty, in *es posible* and *es probable*, the MMP appears together with the modal meaning evaluative. With these expressions, the speaker does not only express his (un)certainty, but also his evaluation of the proposition that is presented in the subordinate clause, i.e. he evaluates it as possible or probable. From this point of view, *es probable* and *es posible* are closer to the expressions of "objective" evaluation such as *es lógico* (*it is logical*) or *es comprensible* (*it is understandable*) (that also select the subjunctive in the subordinate clause) than to the adverbs of potentiality. The co-appearance of the MM evaluative translates inevitably into different mood selection in the subordinate clause: while the modal congruence with the MMP is rather loosened, the MME requires the subjunctive almost always, the presence of this MM opens a wide field for the use of the subjunctive.[29]

2.3.2 VERBS EXPRESSING POTENTIALITY

Predicates that express the MMP, allowing, thus, the use of the subjunctive in the dictum can be divided into two categories:
1) LPs allowing the subjunctive both in affirmative and negated form: *creer* (*to believe*), *suponer* (*to suppose*), *sospechar* (*to suspect*) etc.
2) LPs allowing the subjunctive only when negated: *no estar seguro* (*not to be sure*), *no saber* (*to not know*) etc.

When analysing these predicates, it is important to consider the grammatical person they appear in. The role of the indicative / subjunctive in the subordinate clause slightly changes when the speaker differs from the subject. In sentences such as *no cree que sea / es cierto* ((*s)he does not believe that is is-subj. / ind. true*) the speaker's perspective differs. In the latter, the speaker expresses his conviction that the proposition of the subordinate clause is truthful (and, therefore, implicitly disagrees with the person that represents the subject of the main clause), when using the subjunctive, the speaker remains neutral and does not express his opinion.

28 Original quotation (the translation is ours): "De hecho, es curioso ver que *es probable / posible* que se correlacionen preferentemente con el subjuntivo mientras que *probablemente y posiblemente* se correlacionan más bien con el indicativo, aunque no se pueda constatar ninguna diferencia semántica notable."
29 In this type of constructions, it is not necessarily the MMP that co-appears with the MME. In expressions such as *es cierto* (*it is certain*), *es seguro* (*it is sure*), *es obvio* (*it is obvious*) etc., it is the MMR that joins the MME and, unlike the MMP, impedes the use of the subjunctive.

We can, thus, observe an external factor that changes the relationship between the MMP and the MMR in those cases where the speaker does not correspond with the subject of the main clause. Since our main goal is to analyse those situations where this relationship remains unaltered, we will concentrate only on those cases where the predicate of the main clause appears in first person for these are the only cases where the mood selection depends only on the level of potentiality (which can be strengthen or debilitated through the alternation indicative / subjunctive in the same way as with adverbs and non-personal expressions of the MMP).

2.3.2.1 LPS THAT ALLOW THE SUBJUNCTIVE IN THEIR AFFIRMATIVE FORM

There is only a limited group of Spanish predicates that have p strong enough to allow the use of the subjunctive in their affirmative form. Zavadil – Čermák (2010: 261) mention the verbs *confiar (to trust)*, *desmentir (to deny)*, *dudar (to doubt)*, *esperar (to hope, to expect)*, *es factible (it is feasible)*, *es inadmisible (it is inadmissible)*, *es posible (it is possible)*, *es probable (it is probable)*, *intuir (to sense)*, *negar (to deny, to refuse)*, *parece (it seems)*, *presumir (to presume)*, *puede ser (it can be)*, *sospechar (to suspect)* and *suponer (to suppose)*.

However, most of these verbs combine the MMP with the modal meaning evaluative (*confiar*, *esperar*, *es factible*, *es probable*, *es posible*, *es inadmisible* – see Chapters 2.3.1.1.2 and 3). The expressions *parece que* and *puede (ser) que* have already been analysed and verbs *dudar*, *desmentir* and *negar* form a special subgroup that expresses the negation or denial of a proposition implicitly, from this point of view, they are closer to the group of verbs that allow the use of the subjunctive in their negated form. The above-mentioned set remains, thus, reduced to only four verbs: *intuir*, *presumir*, *sospechar* and *suponer*. In the following pages, the forms *intuyo que (I sense that)*, *presumo que (I presume that)*, *(me) sospecho que (I suspect that)* and *supongo que (I suppose that)* will be analysed together with *yo creo que (I believe that)* and *(me) imagino que (I imagine that)* that in some grammars also appear in the list of verbs that allow the use of the subjunctive in their affirmative form (see, for example, Sastre Ruano 1997: 79–81).

Grammars also mention higher frequency of the subjunctive after the imperative forms of *imaginar(se)* and *suponer* (see Porto Dapena 1991: 128) which led us to the inclusion of forms *imagina / imagínate (imagine* – 2nd person sg. imperative) and *supongamos (let's suppose*, 1st person pl. imperative) *que* into our analysis.[30] Even though these forms are not in the first person singular, the relationship between the MMP and the MMR remains unaltered because the proposition of the subordinate clause is still subjected only to the opinion of the speaker.

---

30 The construction *supón que* (*suppose that* – 2nd person sg. imperative) had only 2 appearances in the corpus.

2.3.2.1.1 CORPUS ANALYSIS

The criteria for selecting relevant data were the same as in the previous chapters. The analysis was conducted in the corpus InterCorp (subcorpus formed by Spanish originals, divided into authors from Spain and Latin America). The analysis took place in March 2017. The verbs *intuir* and *presumir* which had a very low number of appearances in InterCorp were also analysed on the CREA a CORPES XXI corpora (all types of written documents, excluding CREA oral and CORPES XXI oral).

All queries had the same analogical form:

[!word="[Nn]o"][word="[Cc]reo"][word="que"]

which directly excluded those cases where the verb was negated.
For the imperative forms, we used the following queries:

[word="[Ii]magina|[Ii]magínate"][word="que"],
[word="[Ss]upongamos"][word="que"].

Consequently, the results were analysed manually, excluding any non-relevant appearances (the criteria being the same as with the previous analyses).

Table 16: Choice of mood after creo que

CREO QUE	Indicative	Subjunctive
	SPAIN	
Almodóvar	21	—
Bécquer	3	—
Cela	33	—
Cercas	19	—
Delibes	13	—
Etxebarría	46	—
Laforet	27	—
Marías	59	—
Marsé	40	—
Martín Santos	12	—
Mendoza	16	—
Moro	17	—
Navarro	38	—

Ortega y Gasset	5	—
Pérez-Reverte	75	—
Sanmartín Fenollera	27	—
Sierra	37	—
Silva	12	—
Torres	9	—
Tusset	44	—
Unamuno	24	1
Vila Matas	13	—
Total for the area	**590**	**1**
LATIN AMERICA		
Allende	163	—
Arenas	10	—
Arriaga	3	—
Benedetti	136	1
Bioy Casares	11	—
Bolaño	259	—
Borges	7	—
Bucay, Silva	38	—
Carpentier	8	—
Coloane	7	—
Cortázar	76	—
Fuentes	30	—
García Márquez	86	—
Gutiérrez	5	—
Chaviano	25	—
Montero	22	—
Onetti	16	—
Quiroga	2	—
Roa Bastos	2	—
Rulfo	2	—
Sabato	31	—
Sacheri	18	—

Sepúlveda	4	—
Valdés	4	—
Vargas Llosa	112	—
Zúñiga Pavlov	27	—
Total for the area	**1104**	**1**
Total	**1694**	**2**

Table 17: Choice of mood after supongo / supongamos que

SUPONGO / SUPONGAMOS QUE	Supongo que		Supongamos que	
	Indicative	Subjunctive	Indicative	Subjunctive
SPAIN				
Almodóvar	3	—	—	—
Bécquer	10	—	—	—
Cunqueiro	—	—	2	—
Delibes	2	—	—	—
Etxebarría	34	—	—	—
Laforet	1	—	—	—
Marías	42	—	—	—
Marsé	14	—	—	—
Martín Santos	1	—	2	—
Mendoza	7	—	—	—
Moro	1	—	1	—
Navarro	18	—	—	—
Ortega y Gasset	2	—	—	—
Pérez-Reverte	62	—	1	1
Sanmartín Fenollera	9	—	—	—
Sierra	15	—	2	—
Silva	1	—	—	—
Torres	7	—	—	—
Tusset	29	—	1	—
Unamuno	4	—	1	—
Vila Matas	3	—	—	—
Total for the area	**265**	**0**	**10**	**1**

LATIN AMERICA			
Allende	110	—	—	—
Benedetti	4	—	—	—
Bioy Casares	1	—	—	—
Bolaño	53	—	5	—
Bucay, Silva	3	—	—	—
Cortázar	30	—	1	—
Fuentes	2	—	—	—
García Márquez	5	—	—	—
Chaviano	1	—	1	—
Montero	2	—	—	—
Onetti	—	—	1	—
Quiroga	1	—	—	—
Roa Bastos	—	—	1	—
Sabato	7	—	1	—
Sacheri	16	—	2	—
Sepúlveda	4	—	—	—
Vargas Llosa	33	—	—	—
Zúñiga Pavlov	8	—	—	—
Total for the area	**280**	**0**	**12**	**0**
Total	**545**	**0**	**22**	**1**

Table 18: Choice of mood after (me) imagino / imagina (imagínate) que

(ME) IMAGINO / IMAGINA (IMAGÍNATE) QUE	(Me) imagino que		Imagina / Imagínate que	
	Indicative	Subjunctive	Indicative	Subjunctive
SPAIN				
Almodóvar	—	—	1	—
Cela	1	—	—	—
Cercas	1	—	—	—
Cunqueiro	1	—	—	—
Delibes	—	—	1	—
Etxebarría	3	—	—	—
Marías	2	—	—	—

Marsé	—	—	2	—
Navarro	2	—	—	—
Pérez-Reverte	30	—	3	—
Sanmartín Fenollera	1	—	—	—
Torres	2	—	—	—
Total for the area	**43**	**0**	**7**	**0**
LATIN AMERICA				
Allende	16	—	—	2
Benedetti	13	—	—	—
Bioy Casares	2	—	—	—
Bolaño	1	—	—	—
Carpentier	3	—	—	—
Cortázar	5	—	1	2
Fuentes	1	—	—	—
García Márquez	—	—	3	1
Chaviano	2	—	1	—
Rulfo	1	—	—	—
Sabato	1	—	1	1
Sepúlveda	1	—	—	—
Vargas Llosa	17	—	—	1
Zúñiga Pavlov	4	—	—	1
Total for the area	**67**	**0**	**6**	**8**
Total	**110**	**0**	**13**	**8**

Table 19: Choice of mood after intuyo que

INTUYO QUE	Indicative	Subjunctive
SPAIN		
Mendoza	1	—
Navarro	2	—
Sierra	1	—
Vila Matas	1	—
Total for the area	**5**	**0**

LATIN AMERICA		
Bolaño	1	0
Total for the area	**1**	**0**
Total	**6**	**0**

Table 20: Choice of mood after intuyo que (CREA and CORPES XXI)

INTUYO QUE on CREA and CORPES XXI	Indicative	Subjunctive
CREA	62	—
CORPES XXI	146	—
Total	**208**	**0**

Table 21: Choice of mood after presumo que

PRESUMO QUE	Indicative	Subjunctive
SPAIN		
Bécquer	1	—
Unamuno	1	—
Total for the area	**2**	**0**
LATIN AMERICA		
Benedetti	3	—
Bolaño	1	—
Borges	1	—
Cortázar	1	—
Total for the area	**6**	**0**
Total	**8**	**0**

Table 22: Choice of mood after presumo que (CREA and CORPES XXI)

PRESUMO QUE on CREA and CORPES XXI	Indicative	Subjunctive
CREA	26	2
CORPES XXI	60	—
Total	**86**	**2**

Table 23: Choice of mood after (me) sospecho que

(ME) SOSPECHO QUE	Indicative	Subjunctive
SPAIN		
Bécquer	1	—
Cela	1	—
Cercas	2	—
Etxebarría	2	—
Mendoza	3	—
Navarro	1	—
Ortega y Gasset	1	—
Pérez-Reverte	4	—
Sierra	1	—
Torres	1	—
Tusset	2	—
Unamuno	—	1
Vila Matas	1	—
Total for the area	20	1
LATIN AMERICA		
Allende	10	—
Bioy Casares	5	1
Bolaño	3	—
Borges	3	—
Cortázar	6	—
Chaviano	2	—
Montero	2	—
Roa Bastos	1	—
Sabato	3	—
Sacheri	5	—
Valdés	1	—
Vargas Llosa	1	—
Total for the area	42	1
Total	62	2

The results clearly prove that, despite the theoretical possibility of using the subjunctive, this mood appears very rarely. The highest frequency of the subjunctive was found with *imaginar(se) que* in its imperative form. Together with *suponer*, this verb forms part of the so-called *creators of universes*. Nowikow (2001: 93) defines them as predicates that "refer to states-of-facts that are imagined and admissible or, in other words, different to our reality at the moment the message is emitted."[31] When used in the imperative form, their potentiality can grow, allowing, thus, the use of the congruential mood. Nevertheless, the analysis proves that its employment is not very common, and the indicative still prevails.

Even rarer was the use of the subjunctive after *creo que*, *presumo que* and *(me) sospecho que*. We haven't found one single use of *intuyo que* + subjunctive. When the subjunctive was used after these expressions, the resulting constructions always accentuated speaker's uncertainty, as shown in the following example:

> ¿Cómo es la diseminación y cuándo se produce? Lo ignoro, pero presumo que sea mediante las aguas fluviales. ¿Qué adaptaciones tiene la semilla para flotar y luego para fijarse en otra roca y germinar? Es poco cuanto sabemos de la biología de los seres vegetales más interesantes del trópico.
> *What is the dissemination like and when is it produced? I do not know that, but I presume that it is-subj. via the fluvial waters. What adaptations has the seed in order to float and then to stick on another rock and germinate? We know little about the biology of the most interesting vegetable beings from the tropics.*
> (RAE: Banco de datos – CREA. 06.04.2017. The English translation is ours.)

It is indisputable that the usage of the subjunctive after *presumo que* is marked. In the given context, its function is to underline the uncertainty which is also supported by the verb *ignorar (to not know)* and two rhetorical questions the author formulates in the text.

Similar explanation can be applied to the use of the subjunctive after *creo que* in the following example where the speaker accentuates the subjectivity of his impression also with *más bien (rather)*:

> No creo que sea un podrido. Más bien creo que sea un tipo con cojones.
> *I don't believe that he is a jerk. I rather believe that he is-subj. a guy who has got balls.*
> (ÚČNK – InterCorp. 06.04.2017. Mario Benedetti – *Gracias por el fuego*, the English translation is ours.)

In conclusion, we may state that the use of a congruential mood after LPs that do not have adverbial character and are not negated (or do not express negation implicitly) is very rare in present day Spanish. The use of the subjunctive is marked in such constructions and its main role is to strengthen the weaker potentiality contained in the LP. The potentiality is generally also enforced by lexical expressions, not only at

---

31   Original quotation (the translation is ours): "se refieren a estados de cosas imaginables y admisibles, o, en otras palabras, diferentes de nuestra realidad en el momento de la emisión del mensaje."

the level of the sentence, but also at the level of a whole utterance. All the expressions analysed in this section belong, therefore, into the interval (1;2>).

2.3.2.2 LPS THAT ALLOW THE SUBJUNCTIVE IN THEIR NEGATIVE FORM

The last group of LPs that will be analysed in this chapter are those that allow the use of the subjunctive when negated.

Some of these verbs gain the MMP only when negated, while in their affirmative form they express the MMR: *no estoy seguro* (*I am not sure*), *no digo* (*I don't say*), *no afirmo que* (*I don't affirm*)... This group includes all the *verba dicendi* and *verba declarandi*, *verba percipiendi* and some of the *verba sciendi*. The corpus analysis was, therefore, limited to the most frequent predicates *no digo que* / *no estoy diciendo que* (*I don't say that* / *I am not saying that*), *no estoy seguro/-a* (*de*) *que* (*I am not sure that*) and *no sabía que* (*I didn't know that*).

The second group is formed by expressions such as *no creer* (*to not believe*), *no intuir* (*to not sense*) etc. As discussed in the previous chapter, in the affirmative form, their p is very weak and the use of the subjunctive in the dictum is marked. The negation strengthens distinctively their potentiality, allowing, thus, dominance of the congruential mood. The analysis was limited to *no creo que* (*I don't believe that*) and *no me parece que* (*it doesn't seem to me that*) for the other expressions that were analysed in the previous chapter had very few appearances in the corpus in their negative form.

The last group is formed by verbs expressing negation implicitly: *dudar* (*to doubt*) *desmentir* (*to deny*) and *negar* (*to deny, to reject*). The analysis had to be limited to *dudar* (*de*) *que* (*to doubt about*) due to insufficient appearances of *desmentir* and *negar* in the corpus. As mentioned previously, these LPs deny the proposition of the subordinate clause and, therefore, are analysed in this section. It is, nevertheless, also interesting to observe the mood selection when they themselves are negated, the choice of mood after *no dudo* (*de*) *que* (*I don't doubt that*) is analysed in Tables 29 and 30.

2.3.2.2.1 CORPUS ANALYSIS

The analyses took place in April 2017, the queries had the following form:

[word="[Nn]o"][word="creo"][word="que"].

They were analogical for *no digo que, no estoy diciendo que, no me parece que* and *no sabía que*. When analysing *no sabía que*, we excluded manually all the cases where *sabía* was not first person singular.[32]

For the expressions *dudo* (*de*) *que* a *no dudo* (*de*) *que* we used the following queries:

[!word="[Nn]o"][word="[Dd]udo"][]{0,1}[word="que"],
[word="[Nn]o"][word="dudo"][]{0,1}[word="que"].

Since there were not sufficient appearances of *no dudo (de) que* in InterCorp, we also analysed this construction in the CORPES XXI and CREA corpora (excluding their oral subcorpora).

No estoy seguro/-a (de) que had the following query:

[word="[Nn]o"][word="estoy"][word="segur."][]{0,1}[word="que"].

Once again, we excluded those cases where the choice of mood could be influenced by other factors (concessive clauses, conditional clauses), the *hablaré* paradigm is analysed as the future indicative, the *hubiera/-se hablado* paradigms were excluded from the results.

Table 24: *Choice of mood after* no estoy seguro/-a (de) que

NO ESTOY SEGURO/-A (DE) QUE	Indicative	Subjunctive
SPAIN		
Almodóvar	—	1
Cercas	—	1
Etxebarría	—	1
Marías	—	2
Marsé	—	1
Moro	—	1
Navarro	—	1
Pérez-Reverte	—	3
Silva	—	1
Torres	—	2
Total for the area	**0**	**14**
LATIN AMERICA		
Benedetti	—	1
García Márquez	—	2
Sabato	—	1
Vargas Llosa	—	1
Total for the area	**0**	**5**
Total	**0**	**19**

Table 25: Choice of mood after no digo que / no estoy diciendo que

NO DIGO QUE / NO ESTOY DICIENDO QUE	Indicative	Subjunctive
SPAIN		
Delibes	—	2
Etxebarría	—	1
Marías	—	1
Marsé	—	2
Mendoza	—	1
Navarro	—	1
Pérez-Reverte	—	2
Sanmartín Fenollera	—	1
Total for the area	**0**	**11**
LATIN AMERICA		
Bolaño	—	5
Bucay, Silva	—	1
Cortázar	—	1
Chaviano	—	1
Fuentes	—	1
Roa Bastos	1	1
Rulfo	1	—
Vargas Llosa	—	2
Total for the area	**2**	**12**
Total	**2**	**23**

Table 26: Choice of mood after no creo que

NO CREO QUE	Indicative	Subjunctive
SPAIN		
Almodóvar	—	5
Cela	—	4
Cercas	—	5
Delibes	—	6
Etxebarría	—	8
Laforet	—	1
Marías	—	31
Marsé	—	5

Mendoza	—	13
Moro	—	7
Navarro	—	7
Ortega y Gasset	1	1
Pérez-Reverte	—	28
Sanmartín Fenollera	—	8
Sierra	—	9
Silva	—	4
Torres	—	6
Tusset	—	12
Unamuno	1	1
Vila Matas	—	1
Total for the area	**2**	**162**
LATIN AMERICA		
Allende	—	30
Arenas	—	5
Arriaga	—	1
Benedetti	—	12
Bioy Caseres	—	3
Bolaño	—	34
Borges	—	1
Bucay, Silva	—	1
Carpentier	—	2
Cortázar	—	27
García Márquez	—	10
Chaviano	—	3
Onetti	—	2
Quiroga	—	1
Roa Bastos	—	3
Rulfo	—	5
Sabato	—	3
Sacheri	—	1
Vargas Llosa	—	42
Zúñiga Pavlov	—	1
Total for the area	**0**	**187**
Total	**2**	**349**

Table 27: *Choice of mood after* no me parece que

NO ME PARECE QUE	Indicative	Subjunctive
SPAIN		
Cela	—	1
Navarro	—	3
Vila Matas	—	1
Total for the area	**0**	**5**
LATIN AMERICA		
Allende	—	2
Cortázar	—	3
García Márquez	—	1
Roa Bastos	—	1
Sabato	—	1
Total for the area	**0**	**8**
Total	**0**	**13**

Table 28: *Choice of mood after* (yo) no sabía que

(YO) NO SABÍA QUE	Indicative	Subjunctive	% IND / SUBJ
SPAIN			
Almodóvar	1	—	
Cela	1	1	
Cunqueiro	1	—	
Delibes	—	1	
Etxebarría	1	—	
Laforet	—	2	
Marías	4	—	
Marsé	3	—	
Mendoza	2	1	
Navarro	2	—	
Pérez-Reverte	3	4	
Sanmartín Fenollera	—	2	
Torres	3	1	

Tusset	1	3	
Total for the area	**22**	**15**	**59.5 / 40.5**
LATIN AMERICA			
Allende	5	3	
Arenas	1	—	
Benedetti	6	1	
Bolaño	4	—	
Cortázar	2	—	
Fuentes	2	—	
García Márquez	3	1	
Montero	3	—	
Onetti	1	—	
Rulfo	1	—	
Vargas Llosa	4	—	
Zúñiga Pavlov	2	—	
Total for the area	**34**	**5**	**87.2 / 12.8**
Total	**56**	**20**	**73.7 / 26.3**

Table 29: Choice of mood after dudo (de) que / no dudo (de) que

DUDO (DE) QUE / NO DUDO (DE) QUE	Dudo (de) que		No dudo (de) que	
	Indicative	Subjunctive	Indicative	Subjunctive
SPAIN				
Cela	—	1	—	—
Etxebarría	—	4	1	—
Marías	—	1	—	—
Marsé	—	1	—	—
Mendoza	—	1	—	—
Ortega y Gasset	—	2	—	—
Pérez-Reverte	—	10	1	—
Sanmartín Fenollera	—	5	—	—
Sierra	—	7	—	—
Silva	—	1	—	—

Tusset	—	2	—	—
Unamuno	—	3	—	1
Total for the area	**0**	**38**	**2**	**1**
LATIN AMERICA				
Allende	—	6	1	—
Bolaño	—	1	—	—
Bioy Casares	—	1	—	—
Bucay, Salinas	—	—	2	—
Carpentier	—	—	—	1
Cortázar	—	3	1	—
García Márquez	—	—	1	2
Gutiérrez	—	1	—	—
Sacheri	—	2	—	—
Vargas Llosa	—	8	—	—
Total for the area	**0**	**22**	**5**	**3**
Total	**0**	**60**	**7**	**4**

Table 30: Choice of mood after no dudo (de) que (CREA and CORPES XXI)

NO DUDO (DE) QUE on CREA and CORPES XXI	Indicative	Subjunctive	% IND / SUBJ
CREA	74	42	63.8 / 36.2
CORPES XXI	112	92	54.9 / 45.1
Total	**186**	**134**	**58.1 / 41.9**

While it might be not very surprising that the negation opens the way for using the subjunctive in Spanish, the question that arises is, why it is so. RAE (2009: 1908–1909) observes:

It has been noted in several studies about the negation and verbal moods that the subjunctive represents in Spanish a marker of the range of negation, more precisely it is a syntactical indication that the negation takes the subordinate clause in its scope. The presence of the subjunctive in _No oí que me estuvieran_ llamando por teléfono [(I did _not_ hear that they _were-subj._ calling me on the phone)] [...] represents a formal marker that the subordinate clause is in the scope of negation [...].

The refusal of the indicative in some contexts, either with verbs of perception or verbs of possession and acquisition of knowledge, is related to the supposition of veracity that is linked to the sentence complement of these verbs when they appear in the present tense. The subjunctive is, thus, the only option in *No sabemos que tenga problemas económicos* [(*We do not know that he has-subj. economic problems*)] or in *No veo que te quede grande la camisa* [(*I do not see that the shirt is-subj. to large for you*)]. If the indicative appeared in these cases, the result would be a logical contradiction, since we would affirm in the subordinate clause something that is presented as false in the main clause.[33]

RAE (2009: 1910) observes the same contradiction with the indicative after *no creo que* and *no me parece que*, since its use "supposes to affirm in the subordinate clause something that was denied in the main clause."[34] For Ridruejo (1999: 3223), similar constructions are ungrammatical:

> When the speaker corresponds to the subject, i.e. when the predicate of the main clause is in first person and in present tense, it is not possible to diversify the commitment regarding the veracity of the asserted proposition and, in that case, the use of the indicative is ungrammatical. [...]
> (20) *No digo que es inteligente [(I do not say that he is-*ind.* intelligent)] [...]
> It would only be grammatical with verbs of communication and, in that case, the utterance would have to be understood as a refusal of a previous one attributed to the speaker by the addressee where the scope of negation affects precisely the subject:
> —Tú dices que Pedro es inteligente. [(You say that Pedro is-*ind.* intelligent)]
> —Yo no digo que Pedro es inteligente. [(I do not say that Pedro is-*ind.* intelligent)]
> (= "Yo no soy el que dice que Pedro es inteligente") [("I am no the one who says that Pedro is intelligent")].[35]

However, none of these affirmations responds clearly to the question why is it precisely the negation that allows the use of the subjunctive after *no creer que* while with the affirmative form, this mood is seldom used.

Let us compare the following sentences:

---

33 Original quotation (the translation is ours): "Se ha señalado en varios estudios sobre la negación y los modos verbales que el subjuntivo constituye en español una marca del ámbito de la negación, más exactamente, un indicio sintáctico de que esta toma bajo su alcance la oración subordinada. Así pues, la presencia del subjuntivo en *No oí que me estuvieran llamando por teléfono* [...] constituye una marca formal de que la subordinada está bajo el alcance de la negación [...].
El rechazo del indicativo en algunos contextos, sea con verbos de percepción o con verbos de posesión o adquisición de conocimiento, está relacionado con la suposición de veracidad que se asocia con el complemento oracional de esos verbos cuando se construyen en presente, así el subjuntivo proporciona la única opción en *No sabemos que tenga problemas económicos* o en *No veo que te quede grande la camisa*. Si se usara el indicativo en estos casos, se incurriría en contradicción lógica, en cuanto que se afirmaría en la subordinada lo que se da por falso en la principal."
34 Original quotation (the translation is ours): "supone afirmar en la oración subordinada lo que se niega en la principal."
35 Original quotation (the translation is ours): "En los casos en que coincide el hablante y el sujeto, esto es, cuando el predicado superior aparece en primera persona y en presente, no es posible diversificar el compromiso sobre la verdad de la proposición aseverada y, en tal caso, el empleo del indicativo resulta agramatical. [...]
(20) *No digo que es inteligente [...]
Sólo sería gramatical con verbos de comunicación y, en tal caso habría de entenderse el enunciado en cuestión como rechazo de otro anterior atribuido por el interlocutor al hablante, en el que el ámbito de la negación afecta precisamente el sujeto:
—Tú dices que Pedro es inteligente.
—Yo no digo que Pedro es inteligente.
(= 'Yo no soy el que dice que Pedro es inteligente')."

(1) Creo que es verdad. (*I believe that it is*-ind. *true.*)
(2) No creo que sea verdad. (*I don't believe that is*-subj. *true.*)

If the indicative can be understood as a mood that confirms the content of the subordinate clause, its use in (1) cannot be explained because its content is not presented as entirely sure. If we defend its use in (1) by claiming that the content is only subjected to doubt, but not completely denied, we cannot justify the use of the subjunctive in (2) because the negated *verbum putandi* cannot deny entirely the content of the subordinate clause either. Furthermore, we have also found rare but not insignificant examples of the use of *creo que* + subjunctive and *no creo que* + indicative. Our claim here is that this discrepancy can be explained via the relationship between the MMR and the MMP.

It has already been proven that the frequency of the use of the subjunctive (i.e. a congruential mood) is directly related to the strength of the seme of potentiality contained in a concrete LP. The corpus analysis clearly proves that verbal LPs (except for non-personal expressions) prefer the indicative in their affirmative form. This suggests that the level of p is lower here. LPs that are negated prefer the subjunctive, this implying higher degree of potentiality. It follows that the negation is one of the means of increasing the potentiality of an LP.

We have already used several times the term *potentiality*, nevertheless, till now we have understood it as a synonym for *uncertainty*. Now it is precise to specify its significance and underline its other aspects. While our understanding of modality is based on Zavadil's concept, the following description of potentiality is entirely ours.[36]

Potentiality cannot be identified entirely with the level of speaker's certainty, this being only one of its crucial aspects. For us, potentiality is a wider concept that also includes the level of likelihood that a certain event or activity will take place. It is also important to bear in mind that we are not talking about any real, objective probability that could be measured according to concrete circumstances. In our understanding of modality as a purely linguistic and not logical category, the level of likelihood is entirely up to the speaker.

Together with the level of (un)certainty and likelihood, potentiality has a third aspect which we shall call "the range of possible realizations."[37] The greater the number of possible realizations of a process, the greater the potentiality. Consequently, the smaller the number of possible realizations that an utterance implies, the smaller its potentiality. This aspect is also closely related to the level of speaker's commitment to the veracity of the presented proposition, since while increasing the number of possible realizations, we also reduce the informational value of an utterance.

Negation is, thus, one of the main instruments for expanding the range of possible realizations. Let's compare a simple example: a mother is asking her son Pablo about the whereabouts of his brother Carlos. For the sake of simplicity, we will consider only

---

36 Zavadil does not provide any extended explanation of this term.
37 We deliberately avoid the term "possible world" which belongs to modal logic.

three locations where Carlos might be: in his room, in the garden or at school. In this situation, the informational value of the following answers is not the same:

(3) Creo que Carlos está en su cuarto. (*I believe that Carlos is*-ind. *in his room.*)
(4) No creo que Carlos esté en su cuarto. (*I don't believe that Carlos is*-subj. *in his room.*)

In (3) Pablo expresses his opinion about where Carlos might be at the moment and he selects from the set of possible locations (three, in our case) only one that he considers the most probable, negating, thus, implicitly the other two (garden and school).

However, with (4) Pablo does not reduce the set of possible locations in the same way, since there are still two possible locations (garden and school) where Carlos might be and Pablo does not formulate any opinion about them.

Both utterances express the MM potential, since in neither of them Pablo claims to know for certain the location of Carlos, nevertheless, (3) includes higher informational value, implying, thus, a greater commitment of the speaker.

Even though this example is very simplified, it reflects the basic functioning of negation in potentiality. In a similar way, Wasa (2002) argues that the preference for the indicative after *a lo mejor* (in opposition to adverbs like *quizá(s)* or *tal vez*) can also be explained by the extent of possibilities that these lexical expressions imply.

Nevertheless, negation, by itself, is not a modal meaning, compare Zavadil (1980: 33):

> Negation could be considered one of modal meanings only if a negated verb could be followed solely by the subjunctive (as observed with expressions of will or evaluation). The possibility of a modal opposition in the dictum implies that the negation by itself cannot determine the modal value of the predication core of the modal part as potential, it solely creates a semantic framework in which both the MM real (indicative) or the MM potential (subjunctive) can be applied in the dictum. This is not a modal congruence in its original meaning. [...]
>
> It is not easy and would not even be correct to distinguish always categorically between those meanings that are clearly modal and those that are not. Like any other linguistic category, modality has its functional centre and a periphery where it partially penetrates other categories. We have observed this with the affectivity and the same applies for negation where we can say that this category is only peripherally modal, partially modal, in short, it stands at the very edge of modal meanings and expressions.[38]

---

38 Original quotation (the translation is ours): "Negaci by bylo oprávněné považovat za význam modální v tom případě, kdyby záporné sloveso modální části připouštělo v diktu výhradně subjunktiv, jako je tomu například u výrazů volních nebo hodnotících. Možnost modální opozice v diktu však svědčí spíš o tom, že negace sama neurčuje modální platnost predikačního jádra modální části jako potenciální, nýbrž pouze vytváří sémantický rámec, v němž se v diktu může uplatnit jak MV reálný (indikativ), tak MV potenciální (subjunktiv). Nejde tu tedy o modální kongruenci ve vlastním slova smyslu. [...] Je nesnadné a bylo by i nesprávné chtít ve všech případech zcela kategoricky oddělovat významy jednoznačně modální od významů jednoznačně nemodálních. Jako každá jazyková kategorie i modalita má své funkční centrum a periférii, v níž se částečně prostupuje s kategoriemi jinými. Setkali jsme se s tím u afektivnosti a platí to i pro negaci, o níž bychom mohli říci, že je pouze periferně modální, částečně modální, zkrátka stojí na okraji systému modálních významů a prostředků."

This is also proven by the fact that negation by itself (without a modalizer) does not influence the choice of mood:

(5) Creo que Carlos no está su cuarto. (*I believe that Carlos is-ind. not in his room.*)

On the other hand, the negation, as a peripheral modal resource, can play a decisive role when strengthening the MM potential. This strengthening does not translate into an obligatory use of the subjunctive, it only makes it the unmarked mood after negated LPs. By using the indicative, the speaker can diminish this potentiality or, in other words, advert that the level of *p* of the modalizer is not as high as could be expected.

2.3.2.2.1.1 *NO ESTOY SEGURO/-A DE QUE, NO DIGO / ESTOY DICIENDO QUE, NO CREO QUE, NO ME PARECE QUE*

Tables 24–27 that analyse the choice of mood after *no estoy seguro/-a de que* (*I am not sure that*), *no digo / no estoy diciendo que* (*I don't say / I am not saying that*), *no creo que* (*I don't believe that*) and *no me parece que* (*it does not seem to me that*) clearly prove that it is the subjunctive that prevails after these expressions. However, rare uses of the indicative also point out the inaccuracy of some general explanations regarding the choice of mood after these modalizers. We found appearances of this mood after *no creo que* and *no digo que* (two cases with each expression), yet its use cannot be justified by the explanation provided by Ridruejo (see above).
The indicative was used in the following contexts:

Odilón y yo éramos sinvergüenzas y lo que tú quieras, y <u>no digo que no llegamos a matar</u> a nadie; pero nunca lo hicimos por tan poco.
Odilón and I were real swines and anything you say and <u>I do not say that we did not kill-ind.</u> anybody, but we never did it for so little.
(ÚČNK – InterCorp. 27.04.2017. Juan Rulfo – *Llano en llamas. Pedro Páramo*, the English translation is ours.)

Vea, Estigarribia, <u>no digo que</u> algún día <u>no he de morir.</u>
Look, Estigarribia, <u>I do not say</u> that one day <u>I do not have</u>-ind. to die.
(ÚČNK – InterCorp. 27.04.2017. Augusto Roa Bastos. *Yo, el supremo*, the English translation is ours.)

La cosa es horrible, pero <u>no creo que exagera</u> la situación efectiva en que van hallándose casi todos los europeos.
The thing is awful, but <u>I do not think that it exaggerates</u>-ind. the actual situation that almost all Europeans have slowly been finding themselves in.
(ÚČNK – InterCorp. 27.04.2017. José Ortega y Gasset – *La rebelión de las masas*, the English translation is ours.)

¡Pues no he de atreverme! Ese pobre don Augusto me parece a mí que no anda bien de la cabeza, y pues ha tenido ese capricho, <u>no creo que debemos</u> molestarle...

I wouldn't dare! It seems to me that this poor don Augusto is not well in the head and so he had this whim,
<u>*I do not believe that we should*-ind.</u> *upset him.*
(ÚČNK – InterCorp. 27.04.2017. Miguel de Unamuno – *Niebla*, the English translation is ours.)

It could not be stated for either of these examples that the indicative is used because the same information was already presented and the indicatives repeats it (as argued by Ridruejo). The role of this mood in the above-cited sentences is to point out the lower degree of certainty. In the first three examples, the indicative increases the level of likelihood, the influence that the negation might have on the modalizer is, thus, diminished (alternatively, we could say that the level of *p* of the modalizer is lower and the indicative serves to bring attention to this fact; an utterance is generally formulated as whole, it is therefore not important which one of these two explanations we shall accept). *No digo que no llegamos a matar* can be paraphrased as: *probablemente llegamos a matar* (*we probably killed*-ind.); *no digo que no he de morir* translates as: *probablemente he de morir* (*I probably must*-ind. *die*); similarly, *no creo que exagera* means: *probablemente no exagera* (*it probably doesn't exaggerate*-ind.)

The marked usage of the indicative in the last example from the set implies an interpretation such as: <u>*no way*</u> *should we upset him* / *we* <u>*definitely*</u> *should not upset him*, i.e. it reduces the spectrum of possible realizations lowering, thus, the level of potentiality.

2.3.2.2.1.2 *(YO) NO SABÍA QUE*

The choice of mood after (*yo*) *no sabía que* (*I didn't know that*) is reflected in Table 28. These constructions differ from the other studied so far because of the past tense which implies that the speaker's opinion could have changed in the meantime. The indicative can be considered unmarked in these cases (it appeared with the frequency of ca. 74% in the corpus), the subjunctive strengthens the potentiality, underlines the uncertainty and ignorance of the speaker in some moment in the past, *no sabía que*, therefore, belongs to the interval (1;2>, while *no sé que* (*I don't know that*) would belong to the interval (2;3>.

In these cases, the subjunctive (with the help of intonation) can elevate the level of uncertainty so as to imply the denial of the veracity of the subordinate clause. Guitart (1990: 327) mentions the irony in sentences like *No sabía que tocaras el piano tan bien* (*I didn't know you played*-subj. *the piano so well*) where the speaker uses the subjunctive to dissociate himself from the content of the subordinate clause and implies that the hearer does no play the piano all that well.

We have found several examples on the corpus that indicate that the choice of mood after *no sabía que* is not arbitrary. The subjunctive here congrues with the strengthened seme of potentiality and, in some cases, it is possible to consider the presence of the MM evaluative which can also, as we mentioned earlier, strengthen the congruence. Compare the following uses of the subjunctive after *no sabía que*:

Eres una tía rara. Rara de narices. <u>No sabía</u> que las mejicanas <u>fuerais</u> así.
You're a strange woman. Really strange. <u>I didn't know that the Mexican women were</u>-subj. <u>like this</u>.
(ÚČNK – InterCorp. 27.04.2017. Arturo Pérez-Reverte – *La reina del sur*, the English translation is ours.)

Y le aclaró a Claudio: "Hijo de estancieros ¿qué te parece?" "Sí, pero disidente," aclaró Ofelia. "¿Cómo es eso?", preguntó Claudio, muerto de risa. "Hasta ahora <u>no sabía que existieran</u> estancieros disidentes. Me imagino que habrán fundado un sindicato."
And he explained to Claudio: "A rancher's son, what do you say?" "Yes, but dissident," explained Ofelia. "How could this be?" asked Claudio, dying of laughter. "Till now, <u>I didn't know that there were</u>-subj. dissident ranchers. They must have formed a labor union, I imagine."
(ÚČNK – InterCorp. 27.04.2017. Mario Benedetti – *Buzón de tiempo*, the English translation is ours.)

El doctor Urbino le replicó sin mirarla: "<u>No sabía</u> que ese tipo <u>fuera</u> poeta."
Doctor Urbino replied without looking at her: "<u>I didn't know that</u> this guy <u>was</u>-subj. a poet."
(ÚČNK – InterCorp. 27.04.2017. Gabriel García Márquez – *El amor en los tiempos del cólera*, the English translation is ours.)

In all these cases, the speaker does not simply express his uncertainty, but also his surprise that might also imply mockery. The corpus analysis does not suggest, however, that the presence of personal evaluation is obligatory for the use of the subjunctive, as proven by the following examples where the presence of the MM evaluative is practically impossible, the subjunctive is used solely to underline the former ignorance, to point out that the speaker had absolutely no idea about something:

Yo <u>no sabía que existieran</u> agentes literarios, la verdad es que, como la mayor parte de los seres normales, tampoco había leído crítica y no sospechaba que los libros se analizan en universidades con la misma seriedad con que se estudian los astros en el firmamento.
<u>I didn't know that there were</u>-subj. literary agents, the truth is that, just like most normal beings, I had not read the critics and had no idea that books are analysed at universities with the same seriousness as stars in the sky.
(ÚČNK – InterCorp. 27.04.2017. Isabel Allende – *Paula*, the English translation is ours.)

—¿Te refieres al lío de Sebastián con su secretaria?
Ya estaba dicho.
—<u>No sabía que</u> tú lo <u>supieras</u>.
—Y yo <u>no sabía que</u> lo <u>supieras</u> tú.
*"Are you talking about Sebastian's affair with his secretary?"
There, it was said.
"I <u>didn't know that you knew</u>-subj."
"And <u>I didn't know that you knew</u>-subj."*
(ÚČNK – InterCorp. 27.04.2017. Pablo Tusset – *Lo mejor que le puede pasar a un cruasán*, the English translation is ours.)

Constructions with *no sabía que*, therefore, stand between this chapter and the following one that analyses the relationship between the MM potential and the MM evaluative.

2.3.2.2.1.3 *DUDO (DE) QUE, NO DUDO (DE) QUE*

The last set of results to be analysed here is presented in Tables 29 and 30 that reflect the choice of mood after *dudo (de) que* (*I doubt that*) and *no dudo (de) que* (*I don't doubt that*).

The clear prevalence of the subjunctive after *dudo (de) que* is not surprising, since *dudar* partially denies the veracity of the proposition presented in the subordinate clause (similarly to negated *creer*). What might seem more interesting, however, is the relatively frequent use of the subjunctive after *no dudo (de) que*. This verb is analysed also by Haverkate (2002: 59) who observes:

> A negative doxastic expression, such as *No creo que venga* ('I do not believe that he will come'), is conceptually equivalent do the affirmative dubitative expression *Dudo de que venga* ('I doubt that he will come'). A similar relationship holds between the negative dubitative expression *No dudo de que viene* ('I do not doubt that he will come') and the affirmative epistemic expression *Estoy seguro de que viene* ('I am sure that he will come').

We agree with the author regarding the relationship between *no creo* and *dudo*, however, we find problematic his affirmation that *no dudo* is conceptually equivalent to *estoy seguro*. If this were true, there would be no logical explanation for the use of the subjunctive after *no dudo (de) que* (this mood appears in almost 42% of all cases that were found in CREA and CORPES XXI). If *no dudar* were synonymous to *estar seguro*, i.e. a lexical expression of the MM real, the subjunctive would have nothing to congrue with.

We propose an explanation for its use based, again, on the combination of modal meanings. While *dudo de que* simply indicates speaker's doubt and can be used in neutral contexts for expressing uncertainty, *no dudo (de) que* does not behave analogically, for its use can imply some previous question (explicit or implicit) that might be formulated as: *¿Acaso dudas de que...?* (*Do you doubt that...?*). Using *no dudo (de) que* the speaker can imply that the proposition of the subordinate clause is not a subject of his doubt or disbelief, in other words, he evaluates this proposition as accepted. This can be observed in the following example:

> "[...] A comienzos de septiembre partiré." En sus palabras vibraba la tristeza. Y también ansiedad por concluir aquella vida truncada. "No dudo de que las autoridades tengan sus razones, pero son muchas generaciones viviendo aquí. Nosotros somos isleños, y nuestra naturaleza es nuestra esencia. Aquí pescábamos, aquí tuvimos nuestros huertos y nuestro patrón, nuestros padres e hijos han nacido donde están nuestros muertos... ¿Por qué quieren arrebatarnos esta propiedad?"
> "I shall leave beginning September." His words vibrated with sadness. Also with a yearning to conclude a life cut short. "I don't doubt that the authorities have-subj. their reasons, but we have lived here for generations. We are islanders and our nature is our essence. We used to fish here, here we had our gardens and our landlords, our fathers and sons have been born where our dead are... Why do they want to take this property from us?
> (RAE. Banco de datos – CORPES XXI. 27.04.2017. César Antonio Molina – *Fuga del amor*, the English translation is ours.)

The example clearly shows that the reason for using *no dudo de que* cannot be found solely in the speaker's necessity to express his certainty, in this context, *no dudo de que* is synonymous to *aceptar* (*to accept*) or *admitir* (*to admit*). These verbs can also be followed both by the indicative or the subjunctive. When followed by the indicative, the utterance expresses the MM real and the speaker simply states a fact, with the subjunctive, these verbs imply the presence of the MM evaluative and the speaker generally only comments on a known fact and presents it as a subject of his (often forced) acceptance. Our proposal here is that *no dudo* (*de*) *que* behaves in the same way and the subjunctive here congrues with the seme of evaluation. It also deserves our attention that *no dudo* (*de*) *que* + subjunctive is often naturally followed by a main clause introduced by *pero* (*but*). This conjunction implies that the information introduced by *no dudo* (*de*) *que* is not the most important one (since it is only subject of speaker's evaluative comment), the main argument is often presented in the second main clause and appears in the indicative, expressing, thus, the MMR. This can be observed also in the following example:

> Bien, yo <u>no dudo de que Stephanie esté embarazada, pero lo que estoy segura es que</u> ese chico no es mi hermano. En conclusión, estoy segura que mi padre no es el padre de ese niño.
> *All right, <u>I don't doubt that Stephanie is-subj. pregnant, but what I am also sure about is</u> that the child is not my brother. In conclusion, I am sure that my father is not the child's father.*
> (RAE – CORPES XXI. 27.04.2017. Luis Jaime García – *¡Ese hombre!; Las treinta monedas*, the English translation is ours.)

This example also clearly shows the semantic difference between *no dudar de que* and *estar seguro*, since these two expressions are put in contrast here. We, therefore, conclude, that the role of negation with *dudo* (*de*) *que* is different to the role it plays with other expressions of potentiality. Since the level of potentiality is maximal with the affirmative form, it cannot be strengthened any further, however, we suggest that the negation must not necessarily diminish the potentiality as a whole, it can simply diminish the informational value of the following proposition, opening, thus, the space for its personal evaluation which translates into the possibility of using the subjunctive (that congrues with the MM evaluative).

2.4 REPRESENTATIONS OF UTTERANCES WITH THE MMR AND THE MMP ON THE AXIS

a) *No creo que se atrevan-subj. a entrar*[39]
  The expression *no creo* belongs to the group of LPs that are almost always followed by the subjunctive when they appear in first person singular and in present tense.

---

39 ÚČNK – InterCorp. 21.08.2017. Isabel Allende – *La casa de los espíritus*.

Its *p* is, therefore, in the interval (2;3>. We cannot claim that the use of the subjunctive would increase its potentiality, since it is the unmarked mood in this context, therefore, *m* = 0. The final position on the axis is in the interval (2;3>.

P / –R

Image 3: No creo que se atrevan a entrar

b) *No creo que debemos-ind. molestarle*[40]

Once more, the expression *no creo* is used. Its *p* is in the interval (2;3>, however, it is followed by the indicative that can be considered as marked member of the opposition in this context and it reduces the level of potentiality of the utterance, therefore: *m* = –1 and the final position on the axis is in the interval (1;2>

P / –R

Image 4: No creo que debemos molestarle

c) *Probablemente le llame-subj.* [41]

Probablemente belongs to the group of expressions that allow the use of the congruential subjunctive, thus, its *p* is higher than 1. Being the indicative the prevailing mood after this expression, its *p* is in the interval (1;2>. If the indicative were used in the example utterance, the final position would also be in this interval, nevertheless, the use of the subjunctive increases the potentiality; *m* = 1. The final position is in the interval (2;3>.

P / –R

Image 5: Probablemente le llame

d) *Estoy segura de que se fueron-ind. algo desconcertados*[42]

This utterance expresses the MM real, its *P* is negative. Reality is explicitly expressed and, thus, strengthened. *R* is in the interval (1;2>, *P* is in the interval <–2;–1).

40   ÚČNK – InterCorp. 21.08.2017. Miguel de Unamuno – *Niebla*.
41   ÚČNK – InterCorp. 21.08.2017. Pedro Almodóvar – *Patty Diphusa y otros textos*.
42   ÚČNK – InterCorp. 21.08.2017. Isabel Allende – *Retrato en sepia*.

P / –R

Image 6: Estoy segura de que se fueron algo desconcertados

For a better illustration, the axis can be reversed in mirror image to show levels according to the level of *R*:

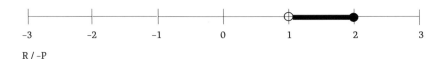

R / –P

Image 7: Estoy segura de que se fueron algo desconcertados

e) A veces pienso que tú no estás-ind. loco[43]

The verb *pensar* expresses potentiality, but in its affirmative form it does not enable the use of the congruential subjunctive, its *p* is, thus, in the interval (0;1>. The indicative has no influence on the final position of the utterance ($m = 0$). *P* is in the interval (0;1>.

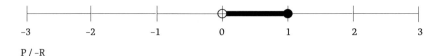

P / –R

Image 8: A veces pienso que tú no estás loco

2.5 CONCLUSION

We have presented relationships between the MM real and the MM potential that can be found in those constructions where other modal meanings or external factors do not interfere. The influence the mood selection has on the level of potentiality / reality was represented on an axis. Scalar representations of modal meanings have a long tradition in works dedicated to modality. Degrees of possibility are mentioned already by Lyons (1986 [1977]: 800):

> If the factuality of an epistemically modalized proposition (as it is presented by the speaker) is of degree 1 it is epistemically necessary; if its factuality is of degree 0 it is epistemically impossible.

---

43   ÚČNK – InterCorp. 21.08.2017. Roberto Bolaño – *Los detectives salvajes.*

> In everyday discourse we do not normally quantify the factuality of the propositions expressed in our utterances by means of a numerical variable. But we can express at least three different degrees of factuality in English by selecting one modal adverb rather than another from a set which includes 'certainly' 'probably' and 'possibly'; and the difference between 'probably' and 'possibly' [...] would seem to correlate, at least roughly, with the difference between a degree of factuality that is greater than [0] and one that is less than 0.5.[44]

We completely agree with Lyons' statement that speakers don't usually have an imaginary axis in their minds where they would position their utterances according to the level of potentiality they express and that this correlation cannot be taken literally. Nevertheless, the axis has proven to be a useful tool to illustrate the relationships between the MMR and the MMP.

We conclude that potentiality in Spanish has sometimes two, sometimes only one aspect (the choice of LP / LR and, in some cases, the following mood selection). The possibility of using the congruential subjunctive depends on the LP and it is not automatic. Even in those cases where the alternation indicative / subjunctive is theoretically possible, the frequency of use of a concrete mood changes according to the selection of a concrete LP. This leads to the conclusion that the analysis of LPs should not be neglected when studying Spanish modality. We claim that there is no reason why the use of the subjunctive should be considered as a priori marked. On the contrary, since the subjunctive is a congruential mood, we must expect the seme of potentiality in the modalizer that enables this congruence. It is only logical that the congruence is stronger when the seme of potentiality is also strengthened. This underlines, again, the interconnection between the mood selection and the characteristics of a concrete modalizer.

It has been observed that some modalizers require the congruential subjunctive less often than others. Throughout this chapter, we have claimed that the overall potentiality of an utterance is influenced by the choice of mood only in those situations where the speaker uses a mood different to the expected one. With those expressions that require or prefer the use of the subjunctive and this mood is generally used by the speakers, we can observe a simple congruence that does not change the level of potentiality (in a similar way, we cannot claim that the use of the subjunctive after expressions of the MM volitive somehow strengthens the volition). The strengthening / weakening of potentiality is possible only in those situations where the marked mood is used after an LP, regardless to whether it is the indicative or the subjunctive.

If we approach the expression of potentiality as a phasal process and the level of p of concrete modalizers as constant, we can claim that the use of the marked mood strengthens (or weakens) the potentiality of an utterance. It is also possible to conceive the level of p of a concrete LP as depending on a concrete communication situation and the whole expression of potentiality as a complex process where different phases

---

44   There is a typing error in the edition we work with. In the passage "that is greater than 0 and one that is less than 0.5" is literally stated: "that is greater than and one that is less than 0.5." We present in the text the modified version of this passage in the form we believe it was originally meant by the author.

cannot be separated. In that case, we can state that the function of the indicative is to underline the lower p level of a concrete modalizer in a concrete situation, while the subjunctive, oppositely, draws attention to the high level of p of the LP it congrues with.

3. MODAL MEANING POTENTIAL →
MODAL MEANING EVALUATIVE

In the previous chapter, we analysed the relationship between the MM real and the MM potential, now we shall concentrate on the combination of potentiality and the MM evaluative (MME) which characterises the content of an utterance as a subject of evaluation. Once again, we will not analyse this category as a whole, our focus here will be those situations where the MME and the MMP influence each other.

The relationship that can be found between the MME and the MMP is different to the relationship between the MMR and the MMP, since the MME and the MMP do not exclude each other and can, therefore, co-appear in one utterance. We have already foreseen some of these cases in the previous chapters when analysing the expressions *es posible que, es probable que, no sabía que, no dudo (de) que*. We could see that in those cases the seme of evaluation strengthens the congruence which translates into higher frequency of the subjunctive in the subordinate clause. However, the question that arises here is whether this relationship can be considered that straightforward and whether there are no other factors that might influence the choice of mood.

The relationship between potentiality and evaluation can be observed on several levels. One of them is represented by constructions with the MME where the expression of evaluation is followed by the indicative in the subordinate clause. These cases are very rare, yet not ungrammatical. The theoretical discussion that accompanies them is, generally, of two kinds.

Zavadil – Čermák (2010: 258) affirm that in a construction such as *Es bueno que vendrá* (*It is good that he will come*-ind.) the seme of reality prevails, the speaker expresses his certainty regarding the future realization. In other words, we might conclude that the MME combines here with the MMR, the latter one being strengthened via the use of the indicative.

A second possible explanation lies in the pragmatic function of the indicative which, according to authors such as Matte Bon (1998, 2005a, 2005b, 2008) or Ahern (2008), can be used to focalize a certain part of an utterance. At this level, the use of the indicative in the above-mentioned example can be seen as a way of underlining the content of the subordinate clause, directing the attention of the listener towards it and presenting the fact that *he will come* as new and important, not only subjected to comment and personal evaluation.

We have some doubts whether this theory can be applied universally to all cases where the indicative and the subjunctive alternate, nevertheless, it is beyond doubt that sentences such as the one we have just commented on can be very clearly explained this way. A similar kind of explanation is also used by RAE (2009: 1882–1883) that uses the term *subjuntivo temático*. However, RAE does not see this kind of interpretation of the opposition indicative / subjunctive as universal and does not relate it to all possible uses of the subjunctive.

We do not exclude any of the above-mentioned explanation and, more importantly, we do not consider them contradictory. Essentially, both explanations are very similar, they just present the situation from different perspective. If a speaker wishes to strengthen the seme of reality, it is clear that the information he presents as real must be in some way underlined, he must draw attention to it. The focalization of this part of his utterance is, thus, a logical consequence of this intention. The first kind of explanation considers the very first intention of the speaker, the second one explains the result of its realization.

A similar explanation applies to predicates such as *admitir* (*to admit*) or *aceptar* (*to accept*), in the previous chapter we argue that also *no dudo (de) que* forms part of this group. These verbs accept both the indicative and the subjunctive in the subordinate clause. With the indicative, the speaker presents the content of the subordinate clause as real, important, informative, with the subjunctive the content of the subordinate clause is subjected to evaluation or personal comment and *admitir*, *aceptar* or *no dudo (de) que* express the MM evaluative.

We can conclude, thus, that in all the above-mentioned constructions we can observe a combination of the MME with the MM real. Since our main goal here is to observe the relationship between the MME and the MM potential, we will concentrate on a different kind of expressions. We will analyse the predicates *esperar* (*to hope, to expect*) and *temer(se)* (*to be afraid, to fear*). The main question we pose here is: What kind of relationship between the MMP and the MME can be found in constructions introduced by these verbs and how is it reflected in the choice of mood in the subordinate clause?

3.1 ESPERAR

The verb *esperar* is a clear example of a predicate that combines potentiality (i.e. the uncertainty whether the content of the proposition presented in the subordinate clause will take place or not) and evaluation (and, possibly, even a seme of will). A sentence such as *Espero que lo hagas* (*I hope that you will do*-subj. *it*) implies not only *I am not entirely sure whether you will do it or not*, but also *I would be happy / content if you did it* (i.e. *I wish you did it*). It is not always easy to draw a clear line between evaluation and will. Several authors mention precisely the seme of volition when analysing the verb *esperar* (comp. Nowikow 2001: 91–93; Ridruejo 1999: 3229). However, we prefer the first possible interpretation (i.e. the coexistence of potentiality and evaluation).

The reason for this lies in the possibility to use the indicative in a subordinate clause introduced by *esperar*. Lexical expressions of the MM volitive (LVs) do not allow the loosening of the modal congruence and if we considered *esperar* as one of LVs, the use of the indicative could not be explained.

Our primary goal here is to determine in what way the seme of evaluation (e) can be combined with p, whether it is possible to determine which one of them prevails and what is the role of the modal congruence in those cases where two MM co-appear in one utterance.

3.1.1 CORPUS ANALYSIS

It is possible to use both the indicative (in its future forms) and the subjunctive after *esperar*, yet, grammars present different explanations regarding the semantic consequences that this alternation has.

School grammars sometimes present the opposition between the subjunctive and the indicative in terms of semantic change between reality and evaluation. *Esperar que* + indicative would then correspond to *wait* or *expect* (or the French verb *attendre*), while *esperar que* + subjunctive would correspond to *hope* (or the French verb *espérer*). However, this explanation is very imprecise and many authors have proven it false, see, for example, Ridruejo (1999: 3229). Similarly, RAE (2009: 1898) observes that "even though '*esperar* + subjunctive' usually corresponds to *espérer* or *hope*, there are frequent cases where it has the meaning of *attendre* or *wait* [...]. On the other hand, '*esperar* + indicative', that is only used with the future tense, normally expresses 'hope.'"[45]

This leaves us with the open question which MM prevails in these expressions. Our approach to the analysis of *esperar* considers the level of potentiality and evaluation in order to determine their relationship in constructions introduced by this verb. First, we analyse the choice of mood after *espero que* (*I hope / expect that*) in the corpus Inter-Corp. The analysis is conducted on the same subcorpus as the previous ones, Spanish is, therefore, always the original language. Later on, we conduct a second analysis on the subcorpus that is formed by English originals and their direct Spanish translations seeking for the answer what kind of English predicates is translated by *esperar que* + indicative / subjunctive and whether a relationship between *hope* – subjunctive and *wait, expect* – indicative can be found. This subcorpus contains a total of 4 144 730 tokens, the list of books that are included in it and names of their Spanish translators can be found in Appendix 2. Since the number of texts that form this subcorpus is much smaller, we formulated the query using lemma, searching, thus, for all possible forms of the verb *esperar*.

Analyses took place in May 2017, queries had the following forms:

---

45 Original quotation (the translation is ours): "aunque '*esperar* + subjuntivo' suele corresponder a *espérer* o *hope*, son frecuentes los casos en los que tiene el sentido de *attendre* o *wait* [...]. A la vez, '*esperar* + indicativo', que solo suele emplearse con futuro, denota normalmente 'esperanza.'"

[!word="[Nn]o"][word="[Ee]spero"][word="que"],
[!word="[Nn]o"][lemma="esperar"][word="que"].

We excluded manually all appearances that did not correspond to our analysis, for example, *espero que sí* (*I hope yes*). When analysing the Spanish translations, we also excluded impersonal constructions *ser de esperar que* (*it is to be expected that*), *se espera que* (*it is expected that*) and the imperative forms of the verb *esperar*.

Table 31: Choice of mood after espero que

ESPERO QUE	Indicative	Subjunctive
Almodóvar	—	3
Cercas	—	1
Delibes	—	—
Etxebarría	—	2
Llamazares	—	1
Marías	—	8
Marsé	1	5
Martín Santos	—	—
Mendoza	1	1
Moro	—	5
Navarro	—	7
Pérez-Reverte	—	37
Sanmartín Fenollera	—	6
Silva	—	1
Torres	—	6
Tusset	—	6
Unamuno	1	1
Vila Matas	—	1
Total for the area	**3**	**91**
Allende	—	23
Arenas	—	4
Benedetti	—	3
Bioy Casares	—	3

Bolaño	—	15
Borges	1	1
Bucay, Salinas	—	4
Coloane	—	1
Cortázar	1	3
Fuentes	—	3
García Márquez	—	7
Montero	—	—
Onetti	—	1
Quiroga	1	—
Roa Bastos	—	1
Rulfo	—	—
Sabato	—	2
Sepúlveda	—	3
Valdés	—	1
Vargas Llosa	—	36
Zúñiga Pavlov	—	2
Total for the area	**3**	**113**
Total	**6**	**204**

Table 32: English expressions that were translated as esperar que + indicative / subjunctive

	ESPERAR QUE	
English respondent	**Indicative (or temporal uses of the conditional)**	**Subjunctive**
Wait	—	33
Await	—	4
Expect	4	90
Trust	1	9
Think	1	4
Suppose	—	1
Count on	—	1
Rely on	—	1
Watch	—	2
Surely	—	1

Hope	13	243
Hopefully	—	4
Give hope	—	1
Look forward	1	2
Wish	—	2
Long	—	1
Want	—	3
Be crazy for	—	1
You'd better	—	3
Imperative	—	3
Total	**20**	**409**

The analyses clearly show the strong preference of this construction for the subjunctive. The contrastive analysis with English also denies that the use of the indicative after *esperar que* would change the meaning of this verb from *hope* to *wait* or *expect*. We have found 127 cases where the English verbs *(a)wait* and *expect* were translated as *esperar* + subjunctive. This suggests that the element of evaluation is not the decisive one in the choice of mood and that the subjunctive does not congrue primarily with e. Another argument that supports this are concrete uses of *esperar que* + indicative / subjunctive. We have found several cases (both among the Spanish originals and the translations) where it was undoubtable that the speaker evaluates positively the future realization of an event and he wishes for it, yet, it was the indicative that appeared in the subordinate clause:

Se trata, qué duda cabe, de una ilegalidad, pero <u>espero que usted no nos denunciará</u>.
It is, of course, an illegal act, but <u>I hope that you will not report</u>-ind. us.
(ÚČNK – InterCorp. 18.05.2017. Eduardo Mendoza - *La verdad sobre el caso Savolta*, the English translation is ours.)

¡Por fin! <u>Espero que</u> de aquí en adelante <u>podré vivir</u> como un hombre cualquiera, que no tiene suspendida sobre su cabeza coronas de muerte.
Finally! <u>I hope that</u> from now on <u>I can</u>-ind. live like a normal person that is not constantly threatened by death.
(ÚČNK – InterCorp. 18.05.2017. Horacio Quiroga - *Cuentos*, the English translation is ours.)

The marriage was slowly unraveling, and we hoped the child would make things perfect.
Nuestro matrimonio se había ido deteriorando poco a poco, y <u>esperábamos que</u> la llegada de la niña lo <u>arreglaría</u>-*cond., temporal use for the future indicative* todo.
(ÚČNK – InterCorp. 18.05.2017. John Grisham - *The Partner*, translation Mercè López.)

Similarly, the following example demonstrates that the use of the subjunctive is possible also in situations where the positive evaluation of a future event is practically impossible, i.e. the level of *e* is very low:

> "So all I've got to <u>wait for</u> now is <u>Snape to steal</u> the Stone," Harry went on feverishly, "then Voldemort will be able to come and finish me off[...]."
> —Así que lo único que tengo que hacer es <u>esperar que Snape robe</u> la Piedra —continuó febrilmente Harry—... Entonces Voldemort podrá venir y terminar conmigo[...].
> (ÚČNK – InterCorp. 18.05.2017. J. K. Rowling - *Harry Potter and the Philosopher's Stone*, translation Alicia Dellepiane.)

We argue that the decision whether to use the indicative or the subjunctive is based primarily on the level of *p* in the above-cited examples (similar observation is made by Haverkate 2002: 101). Generally, it is impossible to strictly separate the element of evaluation and the element of potentiality and their combination makes it natural to use the subjunctive, the following sentences being an example of these unmarked and most common uses of *esperar que*:

> <u>Espero que no sufriera</u> tanto en su infancia como la otra Aline Gauguin.
> *I hope that she did not suffer-subj. in her childhood as much as the other Alice Gaugin.*
> (ÚČNK – InterCorp. 18.05.2017. Mario Vargas Llosa - *El paraíso en la otra esquina*, the English translation is ours.)

> Celos. Quien no los ha sentido no puede saber cuánto duelen ni imaginar las locuras que se cometen en su nombre. En mis treinta años de vida los he sufrido solamente aquella vez, pero fue tan brutal la quemadura que las cicatrices no se han borrado y <u>espero que no se borren nunca</u>, como un recordatorio para evitarlos en el futuro.
> *Jealousy. Who has not felt it cannot know how much it hurts or imagine the crazy things one does in its name. In the thirty years of my life I have suffered it only that one time, but the burn was so brutal that the scars have not disappeared and <u>I hope that they will never disappear-subj.</u> and stay as a reminder to avoid them in the future.*
> (ÚČNK – InterCorp. 18.05.2017. Isabel Allende - *Retrato en sepia*, the English translation is ours.)

Previously cited examples prove that it is possible to strengthen or debilitate both *e* and *p*. While the lowering of *e* did not affect the use of the subjunctive in the subordinate clause, the elimination (or strong weakening) of *p* translated into the use of the indicative in the subordinate clause. Based on these facts, our conclusion is that *esperar que* behaves similarly to *es posible* or *es probable que*. While being an expression of potentiality, the simultaneous presence of the MME strengthens the congruence of this predicate and makes the subjunctive the unmarked mood in the subordinate clause. The statement that *esperar que* does not express primarily the MME is proven both by the relatively high frequency of the use of the indicative (which very rarely appears after "prototypical" LEs) and by the fact that its sole presence (without a sufficiently high level of *p*) did not maintain the congruence with the subjunctive and it was the indicative that appeared in the subordinate clause. We conclude, thus, that the evaluation has here a role similar to the negation with expressions of potentiality: it strengthens the congruence, but, by itself, it does not create it.

3.2 *TEMER(SE)*

The verb *temer(se)* can be considered an opposite of *esperar*. Both predicates present the event of the subordinate clause as uncertain and they also imply personal evaluation. While with *esperar* the uncertain event is evaluated positively, *temer(se)* expresses a negative feeling or displeasure.

Once again, linguists do not unanimously agree whether *temer(se)* is an expression of potentiality (uncertainty) or personal evaluation. For RAE (2009: 1896), it is the emotionality that stands at the first place: "Fear represents, by all means, a type of emotion. The use of the subjunctive in the sentence complement of the verb *temer* is, thus, entirely expectable."[46] However, as observed by Haverkate (2002: 102–103), the expressions of evaluation or emotion that are followed by the subjunctive generally comment upon an event that is considered real:

> [T]he subject of *temer(se)* is attributed both an emotional and a dubitative attitude towards the content of the embedded proposition. [...] Obviously, the state of affairs described by the *que* clause is not real, but a hypothetical one. Although the speaker of the sentence adopts a negative propositional attitude, the subjunctive in the subordinate clause is not triggered by his/her expressing an emotional evaluation, as that would require reference not to a hypothetical state of affairs, but to a state of affairs presupposed to be real. In other words, it is the *potentialis* interpretation of the embedded proposition which explains the use of the subjunctive.

We do not agree entirely with either of the above-cited interpretations. We consider completely relevant the claim that the uncertain realization of the embedded event makes it impossible to see these constructions in the same way as other utterances with the MME, nevertheless, the assertion that the subjunctive congrues solely with potentiality is problematic for the very same reasons as with *esperar*: its frequency is much higher than with other LPs that are not negated.

The situation with the verb *temer(se)* is even more complicated than with *esperar*, for it can appear both as pronominal *temerse* and non-pronominal *temer* whilst the choice between these two alternatives influences the choice of mood in the dictum, being the subjunctive more frequent with the non-pronominal variant.

---

46   Original quoatation (the translation is ours): "El temor constituye, sin duda, un tipo de emoción. El empleo del subjuntivo en el complemento oracional del verbo *temer* es, por tanto, enteramente esperable."

3.2.1 CORPUS ANALYSIS

The analysis took place in May 2017, we analysed the choice of mood after the verb *te-mer(se)* in first person singular, present tense. We analysed both the non-pronominal *temo que* (*I am afraid*) and the pronominal *me temo que* (*I am afraid*). Queries had the following forms:

[!word="[Mm]e"][word="[Tt]emo"][word="que"],[47]
[word="[Mm]e"][word="temo"][word="que"].

Table 33: Choice of mood after (me) temo que

(ME) TEMO QUE	Temo que		Me temo que	
	Indicative	Subjunctive	Indicative	Subjunctive
SPAIN				
Cela	—	—	—	2
Cercas	—	—	2	—
Cunqueiro	—	1	1	—
Etxebarría	2	—	4	—
Marías	1	—	6	1
Marsé	—	1	1	—
Mendoza	—	2	1	—
Moro	—	1	4	1
Navarro	1	2	2	—
Ortega y Gasset	—	1	—	—
Pérez-Reverte	—	1	16	1
Sanmartín Fenollera	—	—	19	—
Sierra	—	—	1	—
Torres	—	1	2	—
Unamuno	1	—	—	2
Vila Matas	—	—	1	—
Total for the area	**5**	**10**	**60**	**7**

---

47   Using this query, the results contained appearances of –*Me temo que*... in direct speech. These cases were filtered manually and they were added to the second concordance.

LATIN AMERICA			
Allende	2	3	22	—
Benedetti	1	—	—	1
Bioy Casares	—	3	—	—
Bolaño	—	—	2	—
Carpentier	—	1	—	—
Cortázar	—	—	—	2
Fuentes	—	1	—	—
Roa Bastos	—	1	—	1
Sabato	—	1	—	—
Sepúlveda	—	—	2	—
Vargas Llosa	1	—	3	6
Total for the area	**4**	**10**	**29**	**10**
Total	**9**	**20**	**89**	**17**

The table clearly proves that pronominal *me temo* and non-pronominal *temo* do not behave in the same way. The distinctively higher frequency of the subjunctive after *temo que* suggests that, whether it is the seme of potentiality or evaluation that this mood congrues with, this seme must be stronger here than with the pronominal variant.

A closer look at concrete constructions containing this modalizer suggests that the choice of mood is influenced by the same factors as with *esperar*. The occurrences can be divided into two large groups:

1) As expected, the largest group is formed by those cases where the semes "potentiality" and "personal evaluation" co-appear in one utterance and their separation is impossible.

> Si hace una tontería, y <u>me temo que la haga</u>, estamos perdidos.
> *If he does something stupid, and <u>I am afraid that he will do-subj. it</u>, we are lost.*
> (ÚČNK – InterCorp. 23.05.2017. Miguel de Unamuno – *Nada menos que todo un hombre*, the English translation is ours.)

> "Ruega por mí esta noche", le dijo. "<u>Temo que sea muy larga</u>."
> *"Pray for me tonight," he told him. "<u>I am afraid that it will be-subj.</u> a very long night."*
> (ÚČNK – InterCorp. 23.05.2017. Gabriel García Márquez – *Del amor y otros demonios*, the English translation is ours.)

2) A less numerous group was formed by those cases where the seme of potentiality was very weak which led to the use of the indicative in the subordinate clause, despite the clear presence of the seme of evaluation:

Eran besos mojados. Me acariciaba la espalda durante horas. Me besaba sin parar. El milagro de los peces y los besos. Más hay cuanto más reparto. Nadie me había besado así antes. <u>Temo que nadie volverá a hacerlo.</u>

Those were wet kisses. He would stroke my back for hours. He would kiss me ceaselessly. The miracle of fish and kisses. The more you give, the more you get. No one had kissed me like that before. <u>I am afraid that no one will do-ind.</u> it again.

(ÚČNK – InterCorp. 23.05.2017. Lucía Etxebarría – *Amor, curiosidad, prozac y dudas*, the English translation is ours.)

Aunque <u>mucho me temo que</u> a mi edad ya no <u>soy</u> una prueba para el celibato de nadie...

Even though <u>I am very much afraid that</u> at my age, <u>I am-ind.</u> no longer a celibacy test for anyone...

(ÚČNK – InterCorp. 23.05.2017. Arturo Pérez Reverte – *La piel del tambor*, the English translation is ours.)

—Es que trato de salvarle, de redimirle de los suyos...
—No, de lo que tratas es de vengarte. ¡Qué vengativo eres! ¡Ni olvidas ni perdonas! <u>Temo que</u> Dios te <u>va a castigar</u>, nos va a castigar...

"I am trying to save him, to save him from his family..."
"No, what you are trying to do is to take revenge. You are so vengeful! You don't forget or forgive! <u>I am afraid that</u> God <u>is going to punish-ind.</u> you, he is going to punish us..."

(ÚČNK – InterCorp. 23.05.2017. Miguel de Unamuno – *Abel Sánchez*, the English translation is ours.)

The analysis of *temer(se)* leads us to conclusions similar to those with *esperar*. Constructions with this modalizer combine *p* and *e*, *p* can be weakened, yet not eliminated completely. The opposition indicative / subjunctive in the dictum serves primarily to distinguish the level of reality / potentiality, the seme of evaluation strengthens this congruence but it does not create it by itself. The lower frequency of the use of the subjunctive after the pronominal *me temo que* suggests a lower level of *p* that can, nevertheless, be increased by using the subjunctive in the subordinate clause (similarly to other expressions of the MMP presented in the previous chapter).

3.3 CONCLUSION

The analysis of constructions that combine the MM potential with the MM evaluative has proven that the subjunctive in the dictum behaves very specifically here and the combination of two modal meanings distinguishes clearly these utterances from those that express solely the MME or the MMP.

Concrete uses of these modalizers show that the subjunctive congrues primarily with the seme of potentiality. However, it is precisely the presence of the seme of evaluation that strengthens the modal character of an utterance and opens a wider space for the use of the subjunctive, its role being here similar to that played by the negation in constructions with the MMP, i.e. it behaves as a peripheral modal meaning that strengthens the congruence. Nevertheless, there is also an important difference between negation and evaluation. Negation contributes on the strengthening of potentiality, while evaluation has no direct influence on the level of p, it exists independently and strengthens the modal character of an utterance as a whole.

This confirms the initial supposition that utterances containing several modal interpretations should always be analysed separately and we should bear in mind their specific role inside the modal system.

4. MODAL MEANING EVALUATIVE → MODAL MEANING VOLITIVE

This chapter is dedicated to relationships that can be found between the modal meaning evaluative (MME) and the modal meaning volitive (MMV). The MM volitive "characterises the content of an utterance (the process of the predicator) as an object of will which can be approached subjectively (an order, a wish, an intention) or objectively (a necessity)" (Zavadil – Čermák 2010: 249).[48]

The expression of will is one of the main pillars of modality in language and it has been, thus, widely discussed in literature. Among all modal meanings, the MMV disposes of the widest range of means of expression. In Spanish, there are several ways to present a process as an object of will:

a) imperative: *¡Abre la ventana! (Open the window!)*
b) desiderative: *¡Que abra la ventana!, ¡Ojalá abra la ventana! (May he open the window!)*
c) lexical expression of will (LV) followed by the subjunctive in the dictum: *¡Quiero que abras la ventana! (I want you to open the window!* literally: *I want that you open-subj. the window!)*
d) modal verb: *Tienes que abrir la ventana! (You have to open the window!)*
e) in the figurative sense, the form of the future indicative can be used: *¡Abrirás la ventana ahora mismo! (You will open the window right now!)*
f) the seme of will is also present in many utterances that formally appear as expressions of the modal meaning interrogative: *¿Puedes abrir la ventana? (Can you open the window?), ¿Por qué no abres la ventana?* (literally: *Why don't you open the window?)*

It is clear that this list does not have to be final and, depending on a concrete communication situation, even an utterance with a completely different modal meaning can be interpreted as an order or request, e.g. an utterance with the MM real *Tengo mucho frío (I am very cold)* that has been pronounced in a room with an open window can be understood as a polite request to close it. Such messages are, nevertheless, undecipherable without being familiar with the communication situation. The question to what extent concrete expressions of will depend on their concrete usage and

---

48 Original quotation (the translation is ours): "charakterizuje obsah výpovědi (děj predikátoru) jako předmět vůle, pojaté buď subjektivně (rozkaz, přání, úmysl), nebo objektivně (nutnost)."

whether it is possible to determine the real content of an utterance without being familiarized with its context belongs to the sphere of pragmatics, we mention some of its aspects in Chapter 5. The upcoming pages will be dedicated to an analysis of lexical expressions of will. We will, nevertheless concentrate on an aspect different to those that are usually mentioned in grammars of Spanish.

Linguists have offered countless attempts to classify lexical expressions of volition (LVs), generally, these classifications consider the following aspects of selection of a concrete LV:[49]

1) Speaker's position with regard to the addressee of his utterance

It is clear that the existence of such a vast range of systemic and non-systemic means of expressing will is related to the fact that very often we want or need someone to do something while we are in no position of simply commanding it. Several classifications of morphological, lexical or even pragmatic means of expressing will are based precisely on the position that the speaker holds with respect to the listener.

A relatively brief, but accurate summary of the situation in Spanish is presented by Hengeveld (1988: 259), who uses a simple axis expressing four degrees of directness that are represented by four model utterances:

   a. ¡Ens[é]ñele su biblioteca! [(Show him / her your library!)]
   b. Quiero que [u]sted le enseñe su biblioteca. [(I want you to show him / her your library!)]
   c. Usted debe enseñarle su biblioteca. [(You should show him / her your library.)]
   d. ¿Puede [u]sted enseñarle su biblioteca? [(Can you show him / her your library?)][50]

From the pragmatic point of view, ways of expressing will in Spanish are studied also by Haverkate (1979: 69) who presents a list of Spanish LVs that are distinguished according to whether they express an order or a request.

2) Semantic characteristics of LVs

This is the second way of approaching different LVs and it is closer to how we understand modality. It is represented by many Spanish grammars that have been quoted here (Sastre Ruano 1997; Ridruejo 1999; RAE 2009). The authors don't take into account situations in which a concrete LP can be used, they rather analyse them according to their semantic vicinity. Sastre Ruano (1997: 63) proposes the following classification:

We distinguish the verbs of *will*, where the features [+ *volition*] [+ *wish*] are predominant, verbs of *influence* characterized by the features [+ *request, council, order, permission, prohibition, obligation,*

---

49   We concentrate here on those classifications that analyse Spanish, universal concepts work with different criteria that are, nevertheless, generally linked to types of modal verbs.
50   The examples are taken from the author, however, in the original, there some minor mistakes in the sentences (missing accent in the word *enséñele*, *usted* is written with capital *U*). We do not copy these imprecisions and present the examples in their correct form. The English translations are ours.

necessity] and verbs of *feeling, appreciation* and *value judgement* by which the speaker expresses his reaction to an event, realized or unrealized.[51]

This way of approaching expressions of will is based on fundaments different to those presented previously, however, in the end concrete expressions of will are again characterized by the level of directness a speaker can express with them. An interesting point is the inclusion of verbs that are labelled as *verbs of feeling, appreciation* and *value judgement* into the list of predicates expressing will. This shows us that the connection between will and evaluation is so close that some authors don't distinguish precisely between the two categories.[52]

3) Subjective and objective expressions of will

This classification (that is presented by Zavadil – Čermák 2010 and was already mentioned in the quotation at the beginning of this chapter) can be combined with the previous one. LVs can be divided into two major groups: expressions of subjective will: *Quiero que lo hagas* (*I want you to do it*) and expressions of objective will: *Es necesario que lo hagas* (*It is necessary that you do it*). From the point of view of mood selection, these two types do not differ (it is the subjunctive, if needed, replaced by the infinitive, that appears in the subordinate clause), however, they are different from the semantic point of view, for in the first case, it is possible to trace the originator of the will, in the latter case, the process presented in the subordinate clause is understood as necessary / convenient / desirable with respect to given circumstances or external conditions, but there is no concrete originator.

4) Presence / absence of an addressee of the will

Analogically to the presence / absence of the originator of will, we can also take into account the presence / absence of an addressee, i.e. the person speaker's will is directed to. This classification is also used by Zavadil (see, for example, Zavadil – Čermák 2010: 252) who distinguishes between the imperative (morphological expression of the MM volitive imperative that expresses the appellative will: *¡Hazlo! – Do it!*) and the desiderative (morphological expression of the MM volitive desiderative that expresses non-appellative will: *¡Que lo haga! – May he do it!*).

---

51 Original quotation (the translation is ours): "Distinguimos entre verbos de *voluntad* –en los que los rasgos [+ *volición*] [+ *deseo*] son predominantes–, verbos de *influencia* caracterizados por los rasgos [+ *ruego, consejo, mandato, permiso, prohibición, obligación, necesidad*] y los verbos de *sentimiento, apreciación y juicio de valor*, con los cuales el hablante expresa su reacción ante un hecho, sucedido o no."

52 See, for this topic, also Chapter 3 where we mentioned that also the verb *esperar* is sometimes treated as a predicate expressing will. Similarly, Kovacci (1992: 46) includes *temer* and *ser preferible* (*to be preferable*) into the group of *predicados volitivos* (*volitive predicates*).

4.1 LVS ACCORDING TO THE LEVEL OF *e*

In this chapter, we present our own classification of LVs which takes into consideration the simultaneous presence of the MME. We base this classification on the fact that the MM volitive and the MM evaluative are very close: if a speaker expresses his will, it is practically impossible to eliminate from the utterance the seme of evaluation of the event that is the object of his will. An utterance such as *Quiero que lo hagas* (*I want you to do it*) could be rephrased as *Me gustaría que lo hicieras* (*I would like it if you did it*).

Also, it is not a coincidence that when looking for an utterance that would be the closest to the construction *Quiero que...* (*I want that...*), we find utterances that also contain the MM potential conditional. Potentiality is another seme that is implicitly present in LVs. If a speaker presents an event as an object of his will, this event must be realized in the future and it is, therefore, more or less uncertain, let's compare the following set: *Quiero que lo hagas ahora mismo* (*I want you to do it right now*) / *Quiero que lo hagas el año que viene* (*I want you to do it the next year*) / **Quiero que lo hicieras ayer* (**I want you to do it yesterday*).

However, being *p* and *e* to a certain extent present in every utterance with the MMV, their level can be very low without this having any influence on the modal meaning and, especially, on the modal congruence that is inviolable in the case of the MM volitive.[53]

Our classification of LVs that express subjective will is based precisely on the level of *e* these expressions contain. It shall present an answer to the question whether this type of classification intersects in any aspects the above presented ones and whether the selection of a concrete LV depends solely on the position of a speaker in relation to the listener or whether the level of *e* has some influence on it to too.

We based our analysis on the classifications presented by Sastre Ruano (1997 – as presented above) and Zavadil – Čermák (2010: 263), who distinguish the expressions of petition (*žádací*), desire (*přací*) and intentions (*intenční*). At the same time, however, we go towards presenting our own classification system based on the criteria we just described. Our classification is represented in Table 34.

---

53   Those cases when the subjunctive is replaced by the infinitive cannot be considered as a loosening of the modal congruence, since the infinitive is a non-finite verbal form that does not express the category of mood and, by itself, it is not a morphological expression of any modal meaning. It can, therefore, substitute both the indicative and the subjunctive. In a sentence such as *Creo saber la verdad* (*I believe to know the truth*) the infinitive could be replaced by the indicative: *Creo que sé la verdad* (*I believe that I know*-ind. *the truth*). A sentence such as *Quiero trabajar* (*I want to work*) means, literally: **Quiero que yo trabaje* (**I want that I work*-subj.), the only difference being that in the latter case, the semi-predicative construction with the infinitive is the only option in Spanish. We can, nevertheless, compare a similar Romanian construction with the subjunctive: *Vreau să lucrez* (*I want to work*, literally: *I want that I work*-subj.)

Table 34: Expressions of will according to the level of e

	Wishes	Petitions and requests	Commands, permissions and prohibitions	Intentions	Causative expressions	Incentives and recommendation
Positive evaluation: *me gustaría que...* (*I would like...*)	**a.** *anhelar* (to long for) *ansiar* (to yearn for)	**a.** *rogar* (to beg) *suplicar* (to implore)	**a.** *imponer* (to impose) *forzar* (to force)	**a.** *luchar por* (to fight for) *esforzarse por* (to try hard)	**a.** -	**a.** *exhortar a* (to exhort)
	b. *desear* (to wish) *necesitar* (to need)	**b.** *insistir* (to insist)	**b.** *ordenar* (to order) *mandar* (to order) *obligar* (to oblige) *exigir* (to demand)	**b.** *empeñarse en* (to endeavour to)	**b.** -	**b.** *animar a* (to encourage)
	c. *querer* (to want)	**c.** *pedir* (to ask for)	**c.** *decir* (to tell)	**c.** *procurar* (to try) *aspirar a* (to aspire to) *pretender* (to intend) *pensar* (to have in mind)	**c.** *conseguir* (to achieve) *lograr* (to achieve)	**c.** *invitar a* (to invite to) *recomendar* (to recommend) *aconsejar* (to advise) *sugerir* (to suggest)
	d. *preferir* (to prefer)	**d.** -	**d.** -	**d.** *intentar* (to try) *tratar* (to try)	**d.** -	**d.** *ayudar a* (to help)
Neutral evaluation: *no me importaría que...* (*I wouldn't mind if...*)			**e.** *facilitar* (to facilitate)		**e.** -	
			f. *consentir* (to allow)		**f.** -	
			g. *permitir* (to allow) *autorizar* (to authorize) *dejar* (to let)		**g.** *causar* (to cause) *hacer* (to make) *suponer* (to imply)	
			h. *tolerar* (to tolerate)		**h.** -	

Negative evaluation: *no me gustaría que* (*I wouldn't like...*)				
	i. *oponerse* (*to be opposed*)	i. -	i. -	i. -
	j. *negarse* (*to refuse*)	j. -	j. -	j. -
	k. *impedir* (*to impede*)	k. *renunciar* (*to resign*)	k. *evitar* (*to avoid*)	k. *desaconsejar* (*to advise against*)
	l. *vetar* (*to veto*) *prohibir* (*to prohibit*)	l. -	l. -	l. -

Table 34 shows that different LVs do contain a different level of *e* that must be reflected also in their selection. The seme *e* in the expressions of will has three basic types: the speaker can evaluate positively the possible realization of the process presented in the dictum, he can assume a neutral position (i.e. he does not impede it or ask for it) or he can present it as something negative (impede it, protest against it).

Transitions between these types are gradual as we can observe, for example, in the column with wishes. It begins with LVs that express a very high level of *e* (*anhelar, ansiar*), at the end of the list stands the verb *preferir* which also contains the seme "positive evaluation of a potential event," nevertheless, it is semantically close to the next group (neutral evaluation) for with this predicate, a speaker expresses that one of the possible ways of realization seems more convenient to him, but he also implies that the other options aren't completely undesirable either.

Compare the following set of model conversations:

(1) A: —¿Quién va a preparar la cena? (Who is going to prepare the dinner?)
    B: —Carlos o Marta. (Carlos or Marta.)
    A: —Pues yo deseo / quiero que sea Marta. (Well, I wish it were Marta / I want it to be Marta.)

(2) A: —¿Quién va a preparar la cena? (Who is going to prepare the dinner?)
    B: —Carlos o Marta. (Carlos or Marta.)
    A: —Pues yo prefiero que sea Marta. (Well, I prefer that it is Marta.)

In both examples, the speaker expresses that the preferable outcome for him would be if the dinner was prepared by Marta. However, (1) also implies that the second option (i.e. that the dinner will be prepared by Carlos) is evaluated in a negative way by the speaker or, at least, it is less acceptable for him than in (2) where he also expresses his will (that it is Marta who prepares the dinner), at the same time, he does not insinuate that the second option would be completely unacceptable.

In a similar way, we can observe that while it is relatively easy to imagine a situation where one could use a sentence like *Prefiero que lo hagas tú, pero no me importa que* lo haga Carlos (*I prefer you to do it, but I don't mind if Carlos does it*), it is more difficult to find a context where a similar construction but with a different LV from the same column would not sound contradictory: *??Quiero que lo hagas tú, pero no me importa que lo haga Carlos (??I want you to do it, but I don't mind if Carlos does it)*.

A more precise interpretation depends on a concrete communication situation and we are aware that the above presented conclusions are simplified to a certain extent. However, it is clear that the main distinguishing element between the LVs *querer* and *preferir* is the level of *e*.

This interpretation is not contradictory to the second possible approach to the situation presented in (1) and (2) that takes into consideration the position of a speaker with respect to the listener. Again, we do not know the context, but (1) implies that the speaker A is in a position to decide who will prepare the dinner. He has, therefore, also the right to express clearly his evaluation of the prospect situation and expect the listener to take it into account.

From this point of view, the example (2) can be interpreted in two ways:

1) The speaker A is in the same position as in (1), but he does not care so much whether it is Marta or Carlos who prepares the dinner. Therefore, the seme *e* is weakened in his utterance.
2) The speaker A is not in a position to decide who will cook, he has, thus, no right to express (even implicitly) his negative evaluation of one of the possible outcomes. He selects a predicate that indicates the course of his will, but he weakens the positive evaluation of one of the possible outcomes for he does not wish to imply that he evaluates negatively the second possibility.

Both approaches to the selection of a concrete LV are closely related and they work in harmony in this case. However, when deciding among other predicates from the same column, such as *ansiar / anhelar* and *querer*, the position of the speaker plays no role in the final decision which one to choose. The selection is based solely on the level of *e*, i.e. on the level of speaker's positive evaluation of the realization of a possible event.

In the above presented example with dinner, the verbs *querer* and *preferir* could be, in certain circumstances, replaced by the verbs *desear* or *necesitar*, however, a similar utterance with verbs such as *ansiar* or *anhelar* seems improbable, for the question who will cook the dinner usually does not cause such a strong emotional reaction that would justify their use.

Similarly, it would be difficult to replace the predicates *ansiar* and *anhelar* in the following examples found at the InterCorp with other LVs from the same group, for they would not express the same level of emotiveness:

> Por fin sale el sol y el oso blando alza una cara transitada y pueril hacia el gongo de miel que <u>vanamente ansía</u>.

Finally, the sun rises and the soft bear raises his rippled and childish face toward the honey gong <u>he yearns in vain for</u>.
(ÚČNK – InterCorp. 17.04.2017. Julio Cortázar – *Historias de cronopios y famas*, the English translation is ours.)

Pero, acaso porque <u>lo anhelo con demasiada intensidad</u>, no puedo llorar y tan sólo logro parpadear con falso énfasis.
But, maybe because <u>I long for it with too much intensity</u>, I cannot cry and I just manage to twinkle with false emphasis.
(ÚČNK – InterCorp. 17.04.2017. Mario Benedetti – *Gracias por el fuego*, the English translation is ours.)

A substitution by the verb *querer* would cause a significant weakening of *e* in the first example, the use of *preferir* seems very improbable in the given context: *??prefiere vanamente* (*??he prefers in vain*).

In the second example, the selection of *preferir* is not possible either because of the low level of *e* that does not permit the completion by the syntagma *con demasiada intensidad*: **lo prefiero con demasiada intensidad* (**I prefer it with too much intensity*). At the cost of a certain weakening of emotionality, it would be, however, possible to use in both constructions the verb *desear*, i.e. an LV with lower *e* than with *ansiar* and *anhelar*, but higher than with *preferir*.

The substitution of *ansiar* and *anhelar* by another LV is, however, inappropriate for one more reason: it would imply a higher level of probability. Both verbs are used in contexts where the realization of the event they introduce is very unlikely. In the first example, this improbability is endorsed by the adverb *vanamente* (*in vain*), in the second example, it is directly denied by the following clause *pero, acaso porque lo anhelo con demasiada intensidad, no puedo llorar* (*but, maybe because I long for it with too much intensity, I cannot cry*).

As we have already mentioned, the seme "potentiality" appears, to various extent, in every utterance with the MMV, together with the semes of will and evaluation. The level of *p* is, in some cases, directly related to the level of *e*, as can be observed in the presented examples. On other occasions, it is, however, completely independent. This can be observed, for example, with the intentional expressions *intentar / tartar* that, in comparison with *luchar / esforzarse por*, contain a relatively low level of *e*, but we cannot claim that the level of *p* is also lower. Comparing the following pair of sentences: *Parecía imposible, pero intentó conseguirlo* (*It seemed impossible, but he tried to achieve it*) / *Parecía imposible, pero luchó por conseguirlo* (*It seemed impossible, but he fought for achieving it*) we can observe that in both cases, the subject, with greater (*luchar por*) or smaller (*intentar*) effort, attempts to achieve something that seems very improbable.

The transitions between neutral and negative evaluation of a hypothetical situation can be also observed when analysing the opposite side of the table, see the column with commands, permissions and prohibitions. Here, we can also follow a gradual change from unequivocally positive evaluation of a potential event (LVs like *imponer*, *mandar*) to neutral evaluation (*facilitar*, *consentir*...). The transition between neutral and negative evaluation is represented by *tolerar*, a predicate that the speaker uses to give his permission to a certain activity (neutral *e*), implying, however, that the event in question is not completely to his liking (negative *e*). See the following examples of the use of this LV:

> Sus padres <u>habían tolerado</u> durante su infancia las fotos de hadas y columpios como un capricho inocente, pero consideraron un riesgo inmenso que luciera ante las cámaras su nuevo porte de mujer.
> *During her childhood, her parents <u>had tolerated</u> photos where she appeared as a fairy or on swings as an innocent whim, but they considered it a great risk that she appeared in front of the cameras as a woman.* (ÚČNK – InterCorp. 18.04.2017. Isabel Allende – *Retrato en sepia*, the English translation is ours.)

> El método de la madre, por ejemplo, podría definirse así: <u>tolerar</u> toda postura e insolencia del niño que moleste a los otros, incluidas las visitas, pero castigar todo gesto o palabra del niño que la moleste a ella personalmente.
> *Their mother's attitude, for example, could be defined this way: <u>to tolerate</u> any child's behavior or insolence that annoys others, including visitors, but to punish any child's gesture or word that bothers her.* (ÚČNK – InterCorp. 18.04.2017. Mario Benedetti – *La tregua*, the English translation is ours.)

In this way, *tolerar* marks the crossing line to the sphere of negative evaluation where the speaker can, again, graduate the level of his disagreement from displeasure or protest (*oponerse, negarse* – lower level of *e*) to a prohibition (*impedir, prohibir* – higher level of *e*), i.e. the opposite to expressions of positive evaluation (*imponer, ordenar, mandar*).

4.2 CONCLUSION

The analysis of lexical expressions with the modal meaning volitive from the point of view of the co-appearance of the seme *e* leads us to the conclusion that there are several factors that play an important role when selecting concrete LV.

We are in no way denying the importance of the speaker's position with regard to the addressee, it is indisputable that this criterion plays an important role in the analysis of utterances with the MMV. Nevertheless, the analysis presented in this chapter has proven that the level of *e* contained in concrete LVs also has a significant influence.

We have also proven that in many cases this is the deciding factor and the role of the MM evaluative in utterances with the MMV turns out to be more important than expected. This confirms the initial presupposition that the MMV and the MME are closely linked and it is impossible to express one's will without the simultaneous presence of *e*.

The relationship between the modal meanings volitive and evaluative can also be influenced by the level of *p* contained in an LV. The mutual blending of different MMs is distinctive here too.

In the introduction to this book, we articulated our main goal which was to study the Spanish modality from the point of view of relationships between modal meanings. In the light of analyses presented so far, we must state that even the concentration on two MMs sometimes proves to be insufficient for a complete understanding of relationships inside the modal system. A closer study of the co-occurrence of three or even more MMs is beyond the limits of this monograph, it seems, nevertheless, that this area, which has not been properly explored so far, presents several possibilities for a future study that might help us understand better the language category of modality.

We followed one more target in this chapter which was to point out the important role of emotionality in the process of expressing one's will. This is an observation that can be applied not only to Spanish modality, but to this language category in general. By highlighting the importance of e in the selection of LV, we are also showing how significant emotionality is for the modal system itself. Its function is irreplaceable and the influence of the MME on utterances with the MMV (either from the point of view of the selection of an LV or from the point of the impact the level of e has on the addressee) is another proof that emotional evaluation belongs to the sphere of modality and we cannot leave it out of account when studying this area.

5. MODAL MEANING VOLITIVE → MODAL MEANING INTERROGATIVE

We will now concentrate on the modal meaning interrogative (MMI) and point out its interconnection with the modal meaning volitive. The modal meaning interrogative "characterises the content of an utterance as an object of an invitation to confirm or complete a piece of information. In its content motivation, the intellectual component blends with the volitive component." (Zavadil – Čermák 2010: 249).[54] The volitive component is, thus, a part of the very definition of the MMI and we will analyze some concrete aspects of their relationship. In conformity with the main objective of this book, our interest will be centred on the lexical specifics of utterances with the MMI.

From the formal point of view, the modal meaning interrogative is distinguished by the absence of a concrete mood that would point out the non-real character of the proposition. In Spanish, this absence is compensated by suprasegmental resources, often also by a change of word order.

From the point of view of significance, the MMI is especially close to modal meanings potential and volitive and this relationship can be, again, observed at various levels and in both directions. Most questions are formulated in order to point out something that we don't know, obtain this information and eliminate, thus, our uncertainty. This explains why the seme of will must be present in every question that a speaker expects to be answered: *¿Estás en casa?* ≈ *Quiero / Necesito saber si estás en casa* (*Are you at home?* ≈ *I want / need to know whether you are at home*). This seme is, though, present also in most rhetorical questions where the speaker does not expect any reaction from the addressee (who is also often absent). Such constructions can be understood and non-addressing expressions of will: *¿Estará en casa? / Me pregunto si está en casa* ≈ *Quisiera saber si está en casa / Ojalá supiera si está en casa* (*Is he at home? / I am asking myself whether he is at home* ≈ *I would like to know if he is at home / I wish I knew whether he is at home*).

Based on the type of the seme of will that is present in an utterance with the MMI, we can, therefore, distinguish between addressing and non-addressing questions, yet we must bear in mind that the difference between them is usually not based on the presence / absence of v (schematically: $+/- v$), but it is similar to the classification presented in the previous chapter, i.e. presence / absence of an addressee which is trans-

---

54 Original quotation (the translation is ours): "charakterizuje obsah výpovědi jako předmět výzvy k potvrzení nebo doplnění informace. V jeho obsahové motivaci se prolíná složka rozumová se složkou volní."

lated into the terms of appellative and non-appellative will. Some aspects related to this type of questions and the simultaneous use of the probabilitive will be analyzed in Chapter 6.

The relationship between will and question can be observed in the opposite direction too. As we have already indicated in the previous part of this book, utterances that formally take the form of a question can be often interpreted as polite requests: *¿Puedes abrir la ventana? / ¿Por qué no abres la ventana?* ≈ *Abre la ventana, por favor* (*Can you open the window? /* literally: *Why don't you open the window?* ≈ *Open the window, please*).

Both aspects of the relationship between the MMI and the MMV can be explored from the pragmatic point of view (with regard to the situation in Spanish, these issues are analysed, for example, by Haverkate 1979, Dumistrescu 1993, Mulder 1993 and Portolés 2004). However, we will adopt a different perspective and concentrate on interrogative sentences introduced by the verb *poder* (*can*). We go towards discovering the role of this modal in questions. This way, we also link this chapter to the last one that is dedicated the polyfunctionality of Spanish modal verbs.

5.1 QUESTIONS INTRODUCED BY *PODER*

The verb *poder* belongs to the group of Spanish modal verbs (see, for this topic, Chapters 1 and 7). In the concept of modality presented by Zavadil, it is defined as an expression of the MM potential possible.

For us, this verb stands between the MMP expressing a possibility, an opportunity: *Puede hacerlo* ≈ *Tiene la capacidad para hacerlo / Es posible que lo haga* (*He can do it* ≈ *He is capable of doing it / It is possible that he will do it*) and the MMV expressing a permission: *Puede hacerlo* ≈ *Tiene el permiso para hacerlo / No está prohibido que lo haga* (*He can do it* ≈ *He has the permission to do it / He is not prohibited to do it*). Silva-Corvalán (1995) proves conclusively that the concrete interpretation of a given use of this modal is often very complicated and both MMs tend to blend. However, we will now be interested especially in the uses of *poder* as a modal element in utterances with the MMI.

Several linguists have observed that many questions introduced by this verb can be interpreted not as inquiries regarding the actual capacity, but as requests. Haverkate (1979: 106) suggests a test where these constructions are followed by *acceder al ruego* (*to accept the petition*): *María le dijo a su amiga: "¿Podrías traerme un vaso de agua?", y esta accedió al ruego* (*María told her friend: "Could you bring me a glass of water?" and she accepted the petition*). However, such a completion requires that we are familiar with the communication situation. A sentence such as: *¿Podrías traerme un vaso de agua?* (*Could you bring me a glass of water?*) does not exclude automatically the second possible interpretation and can be also understood as *Are you capable of bringing me a glass of water?*, i.e. *Do you have a glass? Is there some water you could pour in it? Are you capable of bringing it to me?...* Our analysis concentrates, therefore, on the question whether there are also other factors in Spanish that might help the listener to determine the function *poder* has in an interrogative sentence, without being familiar with the communication situation.

The default typology of analysed utterances is as follows:

A **Polite request (MMV prevails):**
   ¿Puedes ayudarme? ≈ Ayúdame, por favor. (Can you help me? ≈ Help me, please.)
B **Inquiry regarding capacity or possibility (MMI prevails):**
   Poder means "to be able to do something / to have a possibility to do something":
   ¿Puedes ayudarme? ≈ ¿Estás capacitado para ayudarme? / ¿Hay algo que te impida que me ayudes? (Can you help me? ≈ Are you capable of helping me? Is there something impeding you to helping me?)
C **Asking for permission (MMI and MMV are in balance):**
   ¿Puedo hacerlo? ≈ ¿Tengo el permiso para hacerlo? (Can I do it? ≈ Do I have the permission to do it?)
D **Double interpretation (MMI a MMV are in balance):**
   ¿Puedes ayudarme? ≈ ¿Estás capacitado para ayudarme? + Ayúdame, por favor. (Can you help me? ≈ Are you capable of helping me? + Help me, please.)

5.1.1 CORPUS ANALYSIS

Once again, we used the corpus InterCorp when analysing interrogative sentences introduced by *poder*. The analysis took place in May 2017 and we used the following query:

[word="¿"][lemma="poder"][tag="VLinf"].

We worked only with the subcorpus formed by Spanish originals and we excluded from the results impersonal expressions such as *puede saberse* (literally: *can it be known*), *podría decirse* (*it could be said*), *podrá ser que* (*it can be that*) etc.

As a result, we obtained 249 relevant appearances that were assigned to one of the above-mentioned interpretation (the decision was also based on a larger context of the utterance). The concrete form of the verb *poder* was also considered in the analysis.

Table 35: Interpretation of interrogative sentences introduced by poder

Interpretation→	A) Polite request	B) Inquiry regarding capacity or possibility	C) Asking for permission	D) Double inter-pretation
Prevailing MM → Form of *poder* ↓	MMV	MMI	MMI + MMV	MMI + MMV
Present tense				
Puedo	1	23	63	5

Puedes	4	15	—	22
Puede (él / ella)	—	4	2	—
Puede (usted)	2	4	—	12
Pueden (ustedes)	—	—	—	1
Pueden (ellos)	—	2	1	—
Past tense				
Podía (yo)	—	7	4	—
Podía (él / ella)	—	8	—	1
Podían (ellos)	—	2	—	—
Podían (ustedes)	—	1	—	—
Pude	—	1	—	—
Pudiste	—	3	—	—
Pudo (él)	—	1	—	—
Pudo (usted)	—	1	—	—
Future tense				
Podré	—	3	2	—
Podrás	—	3	—	1
Podrá (él / ella)	—	1	—	—
Podrá (usted)	—	—	—	1
Podremos	—	2	—	2
Podrán (ellos)	—	6	—	—
Conditional				
Podría (yo)	—	3	1	—
Podrías	4	3	—	5
Podría (usted)	5	4	—	2
Podríamos	1	1	2	2
Podrían (ellos)	—	3	—	—
Podrían (ustedes)	—	—	—	1
Podían (ustedes)[55]	—	—	1	—
Total	**17**	**101**	**76**	**55**
%	**6.8**	**40.6**	**30.5**	**22.1**

Our analysis revealed that, despite our initial expectations, the unambiguous interpretation "polite request" was not very frequent. From the whole concordance, only 17 cases (i.e. less than 7%) clearly expressed speaker's will and the interrogative

---

55 The imperfect substitutes the conditional here.

element was purely formal. It is not a coincidence that in most of these cases, the subject was *tú* (*you*) or *usted* (*you* – formal), in approximately 50% of cases, the politeness was supported also by the conditional:

> ¿Querrías hacerme otro favor? ¿Podrías entrar un momento conmigo en el Conservatorio?
> *Would you do me another favour? Can-cond. you come with me for a moment to the consevartory?*
> (ÚČNK – InterCorp. 24.05.2017. Juan Marsé – *Caligrafía de los sueños*, the English translation is ours.)

The basic characteristics of will that cannot relate to processes that have already taken place explains why this interpretation was not possible when the verb *poder* was in the past tense. It is, nevertheless, interesting that this interpretation was not possible in any case where *poder* appeared in the future tense (we found only 4 cases that could be attributed to double interpretation). This suggests a higher level of formalization of these constructions where *poder* stands for an LV such as *querer* (*to want*), which generally also appears in the present tense:

(1) **Quiero** que me traigas un vaso de agua.
   (**I want**-pres. *you to bring me a glass of water.*)
(2) ¿**Puedes** traerme un vaso de agua?
   (**Can**-pres. ***you*** *bring me a glass of water?*)

When analysed more closely, both sentences are similar, this similarity being disguised, however, by the semi-predicative construction in (2). It would be more striking if we had the possibility of using the subjunctive **¿Puedes que me traigas un vaso de agua? (literally: *Can you that you bring-subj. me a glass of water?*).[56]
When represented schematically, both constructions have the following form:

$$V_{1 \text{ present indicative}} + (que) + V_{2 \text{ infinitive / subjunctive referring to future}}$$

The main difference lays in the change of perspective the object of will (*to bring a glass of water*) is presented from. In (1), it is subordinated to the verb *querer* which is used in the 1st person singular, referring, thus, to the speaker. In (2) the object of will is subordinated to *poder* in second person that refers to the addressee, underlining, thus, the possibility of choice.

The second possible interpretation, i.e. an inquiry regarding someone's capacity or ability, surprisingly, proved to be the most common one. It clearly prevailed in those cases where *poder* appeared in the past tense, i.e. situations that impede a volitive interpretation.

---

56   Compare, for example, an analogical Romanian construction *Poți să-mi aduci un pahar cu apă?* (*Can you bring me a glass of water?* literally: *Can you that you bring-subj. me a glass of water?*) where the subjunctive can appear.

No sólo los cadetes imitaban al teniente Gamboa: como él, Huarina había adoptado la posición de firmes para citar el reglamento. Pero con esas manos delicadas y ese bigote ridículo, una manchita negra colgada de la nariz, ¿podía engañar a alguien?
It wasn't just the cadets who imitated lieutenant Gamboa: just like him, Huarina had taken the firm position to cite the code of conduct. But with those delicate hands and that ridiculous mustache, a black spot hanging from his nose, could he fool anybody?
(ÚČNK – InterCorp. 24.05.2017. Mario Vargas Llosa – *La ciudad y los perros*, the English translation is ours.)

This interpretation was also relatively frequent with constructions introduced by *puedes* (2nd person sg., present tense), especially when followed by verbs referring to a mental or physical capacity / activity:

Venga, levántate, coño... si sólo te han rozado... ¿puedes andar?
Come on, stand up, damn it... they just braised you... can you walk?
(ÚČNK – InterCorp. 24.05.2017. Pedro Almodóvar – *Todo sobre mi madre*, the English translation is ours.)

La música bullía dentro de mí, galopaba por mis venas, contenía el mundo, y dentro del mundo a mí misma, a mi verdadero yo que había permanecido dormido allí dentro tantos años y acababa de despertar furioso, emborrachado de entusiasmo. Cristina, ¿puedes entender esto?
The music bustled inside of me, it galloped trough my veins, it contained the whole world and myself inside the world, my true self that had been sleeping there for so many years and had just woken up furious, drunk with enthusiasm. Cristina, can you understand it?
(ÚČNK – InterCorp. 24.05.2017. Lucía Etxebarría – *Amor, curiosidad, prozac y dudas*, the English translation is ours.)

The third kind of interpretation – asking for permission – was, as expected, generally found with *poder* in the first person (singlur or plural) in present tense or conditional:

Perdón. ¿Puedo sentarme aquí, contigo, a terminar esta cerveza?
Sorry, may I sit here, with you, and finish my beer?
(ÚČNK – InterCorp. 24.05.2017. Mario Benedetti – *Buzón de tiempo*, the English translation is ours.)

Tenemos que llegar a La Coruña, a ver si allí podemos embarcarnos a América pero aún nos falta la mitad del camino y el invierno nos muerde los talones. ¿Podríamos seguir viaje con vosotros?
We must get to La Coruña, we hope to embark there to go to America, but we still have half of the journey in front of us and the winter is coming soon. Can-cond. we travel with you?
(ÚČNK – InterCorp. 24.05.2017. Isabel Allende – *El Zorro*, the English translation is ours.)

The last type, defined as "double interpretation" in our classification, was, once again, found especially with the verbal persons *tú* and *usted*. We classify as D any appearance where it is not possible to decide whether the speaker expresses his will or he formulates a question. However, the fact that it is impossible to determine which of these interpretations is correct, cannot be, generally, attributed to insufficient context. In most cases, the analysed sentences include deliberately both readings:

Partiendo de que no sé qué demonios es esa Fortaleza de la que habla, ¿puede decirme de forma inteligible por qué se nos retiene aquí? [...]
Digamos que saben ustedes demasiado. ¿Le parece esto lo suficientemente inteligible?
Since we don't know what the hell this Fortitutude you talk about is, can you tell me in an intelligible manner why we are being held here? [...]
Let's say you know too much. Does this seem sufficiently intelligible to you?
(ÚČNK – InterCorp. 24.05.2017. Pablo Tusset – *Lo mejor que le puede pasar a un cruasán*, the English translation is ours.)

In the above-cited example, the construction *¿puede decirme de forma inteligible por qué se nos retiene aquí?* can be interpreted in two ways:

1) *Díganos por qué se nos retiene aquí* (*Tell us why we are being held here*), request with MMV.
2) *¿Es capaz de decirnos de forma inteligible por qué se nos retiene aquí? ¿Existen motivos inteligibles para nuestra retención?* (*Are you capable of telling us in an intelligible way why we are being held here? Are there any intelligible reasons for our retention?*), inquiry regarding capacity or possibility with MMI.

Both readings are included in one sentence which is also reflected in the addressee's reaction. He accommodates the implicit petition *Tell us why we are being retained here* by responding *Let's say you know too much* and, at the same time, he answers the question whether he is capable of formulating the reasons in an intelligible way (*Does this seem sufficiently intelligible to you?*). This intentional ambiguousness that Spanish modals can express is also observed by Silva-Corvalán (1995: 100) who summarizes her observations in the following way: "speakers themselves may not intend to communicate one message to the exclusion of all other possible ones compatible with a given context of occurrence."

While the fact that this kind of interpretation prevails with constructions introduced by *(usted) puede / podría* a *(tú) puedes / podrías* is not very surprising, its high frequency is interesting.

Type D was also, to a lesser extent, chosen as the interpretation of some sentences introduced by *poder* in first person. Ambiguity was, again, the speaker's goal and it didn't result from insufficient context. Nevertheless, types of reading that combined here were different to the previous case. The construction *¿Puedo...?* was, at the same time, an inquiry regarding a possibility (*are there any obstacles impeding the realization of...?*) and a request for a permission (*may I...?*).

—No necesitan apuntarnos —dijo la señora d'Harcourt, adelantándose—. No estamos armados y tampoco vamos a escapar. ¿Puedo hablar con el jefe? Para explicarle qué hacemos aquí.

"You don't need to point your guns at us," said Mrs. d'Harcourt stepping forward. "We are not armed and we don't plan to escape either. <u>Can (May) I speak to the commander?</u> To explain to him what we are doing here."
(ÚČNK – InterCorp. 24.05.2017. Mario Vargas Llosa – *Lituma en los Andes*, the English translation is ours.)[57]

Our analysis has proven that the concrete form of the verb *poder* has a significant influence on the interpretation of a concrete interrogative sentence (this influence proved to be higher than we had initially expected). This implies that the above-mentioned types of interpretation are not realized at random and do not depend solely on a concrete communication situation. On the contrary, they are strongly linked to concrete forms of *poder* which makes it easier for the addressee to react appropriately to a given utterance.

Nevertheless, it is undoubtable that verbal person, mood and time of *poder* are not sufficient for a clear distinction between different interpretations. This can be observed especially with sentences introduced by *puedes* that permitted, systematically, two kinds of reading: "inquiry regarding capacity or possibility" and "double interpretation." Similarly, with *puedo* there were two frequent interpretations: "inquiry regarding capacity or possibility" and "asking for permission." This suggests that there must be some other factors that help the addressee to decipher correctly a concrete utterance. To determine these factors, we subjected the initial concordance obtained from the corpus to a second analysis that concentrated on the kind of infinitives that generally appear after *poder* in these constructions.

5.1.2 CORPUS ANALYSIS N. 2

We analysed all the uses of *poder* in interrogative constructions we had obtained in the first phase. We considered only those infinitives that had a frequency ≥ 5. We excluded the polyfunctional verb *hacer* (*to do, to make*) that had several interpretations.

---

57 In these cases, the distinction between type A and D was the hardest one. When choosing the interpretation, we considered the larger context of each utterance, especially whether it was plausible that there might be any objective obstacles or whether, according to the context, the decision lied entirely on the addressee.
In a sentence like: *¿Puedo hablar con el jefe?* it is possible to imagine several objective reasons that might impede speaking to the commander and cannot be attributed to the addressee (the commander not being present, the commander not willing to talk to anyone...). Therefore, we chose the interpretation D here.
On the other hand, with a sentence like *¿Puedo sentarme aquí, contigo, a terminar esta cerveza?* that was mentioned among those that were interpreted as A, we do not see any objective reasons that might impede the speaker's wish and we attribute the decision entirely to the addressee, since there is no third person that needs to be considered.
We also choose the interpretation A when the speaker explicitly added any lexical expression of will or otherwise clearly indicated the volitive interpretation of his utterance, for example, by using *por favor* (*please*).

Table 36: *Interpretation of interrogative constructions introduced by* poder

Interpretation→	A) Polite request	B) Inquiry regarding capacity or possibility	C) Asking for permission	D) Double interpretation
Prevailing MM→ Infinitive following poder ↓	MMV	MMI	MMI + MMV	MMI + MMV
Ayudar (to help)	1	1	—	9
Conseguir (to achieve)	—	3	—	—
Contar con alguien / con algo (to count on someone / something)	—	3	—	—
Decir (to say, to tell)	—	—	—	18
Explicar (to explain)	—	—	—	6
Hablar (to speak)	—	3	—	4
Imaginar (to imagine)	—	4	—	—
Ir (to go)	—	1	6	1
Irse (to leave)	—	2	6	—
Llamar (to call)	—	—	5	1
Llevar (to take, to carry)	—	1	—	4
Pasar (to pass)	—	—	3	—
Pedir (to ask for)	—	1	3	—
Preguntar (to ask)	—	—	6	—
Quedarse (to stay)	—	1	2	1
Resistir (to resist)	—	3	—	—
Seguir* (to follow, to continue)	—	3	1	—
Sentarse (to sit down)	—	—	3	—
Ver (to see)	—	4	2	2
Total	**1**	**30**	**38**	**45**

* We excluded manually those cases where *seguir* formed part of a periphrastic construction.

This analysis has proven to be an effective tool to determine the correct interpretation. The results clearly reveal that the interpretation depends to a large extent on the semantics of the infinitive that follows the verb *poder*.

In some cases, one type of interpretation was the only one that could be found with a concrete verb. This can be observed with *verba dicendi* such as *decir* and *explicar* that always appeared in constructions with double interpretation that combined the MMI (*are you capable of telling / explaining...?*) with the MMV (*tell me / explain to me*):

> El padre Yves observó a Marco Valoni antes de preguntarle.
> —Perdón, señor Valoni, pero ¿podría decirme qué busca?
> —Padre Yves, ni el señor Valoni sabe lo que busca, pero el caso es que quiere saber quién ha tenido relación con la Síndone en los últimos veinte años y nosotros se lo vamos a facilitar.
> *Father Yves observed Marco Valoni before asking.*
> *"Excuse me, Mr. Valoni, but could you tell me what you are looking for?"*
> *"Father Yves, not even Mr. Valoni knows what he is looking for, but he wants to know who has been in contact with the Síndone in the last twenty years and we shall facilitate it."*
> (ÚČNK – InterCorp. 30.05.2017. Julia Navarro – *La Hermandad de la Sábana Santa*, the English translation is ours.)

When combined with *poder* in first person, constructions with *verba dicendi* could certainly be interpreted as type C – asking for permission: ¿*puedo decirlo?* (*May / Can I say it?* ≈ *Do you give me the permission to say it?*), nevertheless, the interpretation B (inquiry regarding capacity or possibility) does not seem plausible under normal circumstances.

The results were unambiguous also with the verb *preguntar* that appeared only in combination with *poder* in first person singular (present tense). The semantics of the infinitive and the verbal person and tense of *poder* were sufficient for an unequivocal interpretation (here, it was the type C – asking for permission).

While *verba dicendi* combined with interpretation types C and D (combination of the MMI and the MMV), verbs that express some physical or mental activity / ability (*conseguir, imaginar, ir(se), resistir, sentarse, ver*) implied generally interpretations B and C / D. It was, once again, the verbal person of *poder* (sometimes also the tense) that helped to determine the type more precisely: first person singular preferred the types C / D, other verbal persons preferred the type B.

Type D (asking for permission + inquiry regarding possibility) – *poder* in first person:

> —Me gustaría darle una explicación a su hija, señor Chien. ¿Puedo verla, por favor?
> —Debo preguntarle a Lynn. Por el momento no desea ver a nadie, pero le haré saber si cambia de opinión —replicó el zhong-yi, acompañándolo a la puerta.
> *"I would like to explain myself to your daughter, Mr. Chien. Can / May I see her, please?"*
> *"I have to ask Lynn. At the moment, she doesn't want to see anybody, but I shall let you know if she changes her mind," replied the zhong-yi, accompanying him to the door.*
> (ÚČNK – InterCorp. 30.05.2017. Isabel Allende – *Retrato en sepia*, the English translation is ours.)

Type B (inquiry regarding capacity / possibility) – *poder* in second person:

> —Soy el Turco, tu hermano, soy Salvador —le dijo, arrastrándose hacia él—. ¿Puedes oírme? ¿Puedes verme, Guaro?

"I am el Turco, your brother, I am Salvador," he said crawling towards him. "<u>Can you hear me? Can you see me, Guaro?</u>"
(ÚČNK – InterCorp. 30.05.2017. Mario Vargas Llosa – *La fiesta del chivo*, the English translation is ours.)

Typ C (asking for permission) – *poder* in present tense:

—Perdóname, papá. Tengo que salir a hacer un encargo. <u>¿Puedo irme?</u>
"Excuse me, dad. I have to go and arrange something. <u>May I leave?</u>"
(ÚČNK – InterCorp. 30.05.2017. Mario Vargas Llosa – *La ciudad y los perros*, the English translation is ours.)

Typ B (inquiry regarding capacity / possibility) – *poder* in past tense:

—¿No ve en qué estado estoy? —gimoteó el miope, señalándose los ojos enrojecidos, saltones, acuosos, huidizos—. ¿No ve que sin anteojos soy un ciego? <u>¿Podía irme solo, dando tumbos por el sertón?</u>
"Can't you see the state I am in?" the short-sighted man whined and pointed at his red, bulging, watery, evasive eyes. "Can't you see that without glasses I am blind? <u>Could I leave by myself and walk for the wasteland?</u>"
(ÚČNK – InterCorp. 30.05.2017. Mario Vargas Llosa – *Guerra del fin del mundo*, the English translation is ours.)

5.2 CONCLUSION

Corpus analyses have proven that the concrete interpretation of interrogative utterances introduced by *poder* can be generally decided even without being familiar with the wider context. It is the verbal person and verbal tense of *poder* and the semantics of the following infinitive that play a decisive role in its determination. The importance of these factors changes depending on a concrete infinitive. There are verbs that primarily offer just one interpretation (for example, the verb *resistir* that combined only with the type B), with others the interpretation changes according the form of *poder*.

Even though the corpus often offers only a limited context, we have not found a single utterance that could not be attributed to one concrete interpretation type. This leads us to the conclusion that the role of a concrete communication situation tends to be slightly overestimated when analysing this type of constructions. We do not claim that in a specific context some of the above-cited utterances could not be interpreted differently, however, this can be said about any utterance regardless of the (non)presence of *poder*.

The analysis has also shown that even when familiarized with the wider context of a concrete utterance, it is often impossible to eliminate completely its ambiguousness and this ambiguity can be interpreted as a speaker's intention, not as a result of insufficient understanding of the communication situation. The corpus analysis has shown many interrogative constructions that required an addressee's reaction to both components of their meaning: the element of will and the element of question / uncertainty.

In the framework of the MM interrogative, the questions introduced by *poder* have a specific role. As we have already stated, every interrogative sentence contains also an element of will, the seme *v* being the main element that differentiates the utterances with the MMP and the MMI. Compare, for example *Creo que está aquí* (*I think he is here*) ≈ *I am not sure whether he is here* and *¿Está aquí?* (*Is he here?*) ≈ *I am not sure whether he is here* + *I want to know whether he is here*. Schematically, the situation can be described as follows: $i = p + v$. The presence of the modalizer *poder* (that, by itself, stands between the MMP and the MMV) can multiply the volitive element and transfer the whole utterance completely into the framework of the MM volitive, however, as proven by the corpus analysis, these cases are not as frequent as it might seem. In most cases, the original interrogative element is maintained.

The classification of utterances according to the prevailing modal meaning (MMV, MMI, MMV + MMI) was relatively simple, a closer analysis of types C and D (MMI + MMV) could probably determine whether it is the element of will or the interrogative element that prevails, nevertheless, eliminating one of them completely proved to be impossible. However, this did not impede addressee's understanding and the following reaction.

This leads us again to the conclusion that a combination of several MMs inside one single utterance is a completely natural phenomenon in language, it appears at all its levels and speakers and addressees can operate with it.

6. MODAL MEANING INTERROGATIVE → MODAL MEANING POTENTIAL

In the following analysis, we will continue our study of specific interrogative utterances. This time, we will concentrate on the relationship between the MM interrogative and the MM potential.

The presence of p in constructions with the MMI was already mentioned in the previous chapter. Consequently, the possibilites of mood selection in the dictum are different than in utterances without the MMI:

(1) Creo que está cansado. (I believe that he is-*ind.* tired.)
(2) ¿Crees que está / esté cansado? (Do you believe that he is-*ind.* / *subj.* tired?)

This phenomenon is analysed in detail by Wasa (1999: 124) who presents a whole set of interrogative constructions introduced by *creer* that are followed by the subjunctive and, also, replies to these questions. His observations lead the author to the conclusion that the main function of this mood is the focalization of the dictum:

> We can observe that in all the replies to (20)-(24), the listener, with no exception, does not reply yes or no, but he expresses his opinion regarding the embedded proposition. The subjunctive indicates that the subordinate clause is the focalized one.[58]

This theory analyses, again, the opposition indicative / subjunctive in terms of emphasizing / weakening the importance of one part of the utterance. Similar approach is presented by Ahern (2008: 37):

> In interrogative sentences, [the subjunctive] is only used in the subordinate clauses that these might contain, its function here is to show more or less subtle notions regarding the focus of the question: it helps us, for example, to determine whether the speaker asks about the content of the main clause or the content of the subordinate one, as can be observed by:

---

58   Original quotation (the translation is ours): "Notamos que en todas las respuestas de (20)-(24), el oyente, sin excepción, no contesta ni sí ni no, sino que expresa su misma opinión sobre la proposición de la subordinada. El subjuntivo nos indica que la subordinada es ahora el foco."

1. ¿Notaste que la niña se pusiera triste? [(Did you notice that the girl got-*subj.* sad?)]
2. ¿Notaste que la niña se puso triste? [(Did you notice that the girl got-*ind.* sad?)]

In (1), we would understand that the speaker wants to know whether the content of the subordinate clause it is true or not (*that the girl got sad*).

In (2), we understand that the speaker does not have any doubts regarding the content of the embedded clause, but he wants to confirm the content of the main clause: yes or no.[59]

Following the interpretation of the subjunctive as a congruential mood which reacts to the presence of semes *p*, *v* and *e* that we defend, we understand the above cited utterances as constructions where the increased uncertainty of the speaker, strengthens the potentiality of the proposition in the subordinate clause that, naturally, accepts the subjunctive. The possibility of its use in an utterance introduced by the LR *notar* (*to notice*) is a proof that the seme *p* is an inherent component of the modal meaning interrogative (the dynamics of the relationship between *i* and *p* are similar to the relationship between potentiality and negation that was described in Chapter 2).

We have also stated already that a specific attribute of the MMI is the absence of its own mood that would be a sign of the presence of *i*. The MMI is, thus, an atypical modal meaning and its connection with other MMs is very distinctive. In order to present clearly the relationship between the MMI and the MMP, we chose a specific type of utterances, concretely the questions introduced by the probabilitive, where we can observe and additional accumulation of both MMs.

6.1 INTERROGATIVE CONSTRUCTIONS WITH THE PROBABILITIVE

Spanish interrogative and declarative utterances differ in the intonation, sometimes also in their word order:

(3) Está en casa. (He is at home.)
(4) ¿Está en casa? (Is he at home?)
(5) Luis está en casa. / ⁇Está Luis en casa. (Luis is at home, / ⁇Is Luis at home.)
(6) Luis está en casa. / ¿Está Luis en casa? (Luis is at home. / Is Luis at home?)

---

59 Original quotation (the translation is ours): "[El subjuntivo] se reserva en las oraciones interrogativas a las oraciones subordinadas que pueden contener, donde cumple una función de mostrar matices más o menos sutiles en relación con el foco de la pregunta: nos ayuda, por ejemplo, a determinar si se está preguntando sobre el contenido se la oración principal, o bien sobre el de la subordinada, como podemos observar en el contraste:
1. ¿Notaste que la niña se pusiera triste?
2. ¿Notaste que la niña se puso triste?
En (1), entenderíamos que lo que el hablante quiere saber es si es verdad o no lo que se expresa en la oración subordinada, *que la niña se pusiera triste*.
En (2), entendemos que el hablante no tiene dudas sobre contenido de la oración subordinada, sino que trata de confirmar lo expresado en la oración principal: sí o no."

There is also a marked variant for (4) and (6) where the speaker uses the probabilitive:

(7) ¿Estará (Luis) en casa? (Is-*prob.* (Luis) at home?)

Let's analyse now the relationship between the following pairs of utterances:

(8) Estará en casa. (He is at home, I suppose. Literally: He is-*prob.* at home.)
(9) ¿Estará en casa? (Could he be at home? Literally: Is-*prob.* he at home?)
(10) Este chico será Luis. (This boy is Luis, I suppose. Literally: This boy is-*prob.* Luis.)
(11) ¿Quién será este chico? (Who could be this boy? Literally: Who is-*prob.* this boy?)

In (8), the proposition content is presented as non-real, but, at the same time, probable (the speaker has reasons to believe the subject is at home). This probability is based on a justifiable assumption (for example, the person in question is almost always at home at this time of the day) or a proof (e.g. a light in the window) and it is expressed via the probabilitive.

The semantic notion of supposition that mention Zavadil – Čermák (2010: 251) with respect to this mood is maintained in (9), i.e. in a polar question, but not in the non-polar question (11) that can be pronounced by a speaker who has absolutely no idea regarding the identity of the boy in question. This leads to the conclusion that the role of the probabilitive in utterances with the MMI must be, at least to a certain extent, different to its function in declarative constructions that express the MM potential probabilitive.

Spanish grammars often mention a rhetorical character of questions introduced by the probabilitive (see, for example, RAE 2009: 1772–1773). The presence / absence of an addressee is also important from the point of view of modality, since it defines the type of the volitive element (will conceived as appellative or non-appellative).

We shall now leave aside the complex typology of interrogative sentences and we will not use terms such as *rhetorical* or *deliberative question*. Since our research is based on other criteria, we choose terms that are analogical to those used with the MMV: *appellative* and *non-appellative question*.

From the point of view of modal meaning, we may state that non-appellative questions with the probabilitive are distinguished by strengthening the seme *p* (the speaker expresses primarily his uncertainty, he does not formulate a question directed to a concrete listener). They also differ from declarative sentences with the MMP by the presence of the element of will (*I want to know...*) that is present in every utterance with the MMI. Let's compare:

(12) Luis estará en casa. ≈ Luis está probablemente en casa.
     (Luis is-*prob.* at home. ≈ Luis is probably at home.)
     MMP probabilitive expressing probability without an element of will.

(13) ¿Dónde está Luis? ≈ **Te** pregunto dónde está Luis.
(Where is-*ind.* Luis? ≈ I am asking **you** where Luis is.)
MMI, the volitive element relates to the addressee of the question, we shall use the term *appellative i* – MMIa

(14) ¿Dónde estará Luis? ≈ **Me** pregunto dónde **puede** estar Luis.
(Where is-*prob.* Luis? ≈ I am asking **myself** where Luis **might** be.)
MMI + MMP, the use of the probabilitive strengthens the *p*, the volitive element is non-appellative – MMInon-a

(15) ¿Dónde estará Luis? ≈ **Te** pregunto dónde **puede** estar Luis.
(Where is-*prob.* Luis? ≈ I am asking **you** where Luis **might** be.)
MMI + MMP, the probabilitive underlines *p*, the volitive element is appellative – MMIa

6.1.1 CORPUS ANALYSIS

The existence / non-existence of an addressee was defined as crucial for the corpus analysis that was conducted on the InterCorp (subcorpus formed by Spanish originals). The analysis took place in August 2017 and it had two phases: in the first one we searched for questions introduced by the *hablará* paradigm (future indicative or present / future probabilitive), in the second phase, we analysed constructions introduced by an interrogative pronoun followed by the probabilitive. The queries had the following form:

[word="¿"][word=".*rá.*|.*ré.*|.*remos"&tag="V.*"],
[word="¿"][tag="INT"][word=".*rá.*|.*ré.*|.*remos"&tag="V.*"].

We manually excluded all non-relevant appearences, we analysed only the *hablará* paradigm and excluded manually the *habré hablado* paradigm (future perfect indicative, past perfect / future perfect probabilitive). Consequently, we analysed in detail all the appearances and their context and we assigned them to one of these two types:

A – non-appellative question (can be paraphrased as *I am asking myself...*)
B – appellative question (can be paraphrased as *I am asking you...*)

We are aware of possible inaccuracies that might appear in the analysis. Often it is impossible to decide whether the *hablará* paradigm functions as the future indicative or as present / future probabilitive. However, our analysis leads us to the conclusion that in the studied constructions there is generally a syncretism of both meanings and modal and temporal shades [+prob] and [+fut] penetrate to the extent that it is impossible to separate them.

The results are resumed in Tables 37 and 38.

Table 37: *Interpretation of interrogative constructions introduced by* hablará

	A **Non-appellative question** MMInon-a + MMPprob (**Me** *pregunto...*)	B **Appellative question** MMIa + MMPprob (**Te** *pregunto...*)
Yo (*I*)	39	5
Tú / Vos (*You – informal, sg.*)	15	32
Él / Ella / Ello (*He / She / It*)	132	17
Usted / Vos (*You – formal, sg.*)	1	15
Nosotros (*We*)	4	7
Vosotros (*You - informal, pl., Spain*)	—	—
Ellos / Ellas (*They*)	27	8
Ustedes (*You – formal, pl., Spain; You – pl., Latin America*)	—	3
Impersonal *Habrá*	6	3
Impersonal *Habrá de*	1	—
Impersonal *Habrá que*	2	—
Total	**227**	**90**
%	**71.6**	**28.4**

Table 38: *Interpretation of interrogative constructions introduced by an interrogative pronoun followed by* hablará

	A **Non-appellative question** MMInon-a + MMPprob (**Me** *pregunto...*)	B **Appellative question** MMIa + MMPprob (**Te** *pregunto...*)
Yo (*I*)	5	—
Tú / Vos (*You – informal, sg.*)	5	2
Él / Ella / Ello (*He / She / It*)	94	12
Usted / Vos (*You – formal, sg.*)	1	2
Nosotros (*We*)	3	1
Vosotros (*You - informal, pl., Spain*)	—	1
Ellos / Ellas (*They*)	7	2
Ustedes (*You – formal, pl., Spain; You – pl., Latin America*)	—	—
Impersonal *habrá*	2	—
Total	**117**	**20**
%	**85.4**	**14.6**

Tables clearly show the predominance of the type A, this confirms the initial presupposition that these constructions function mainly as non-appellative questions that do not expect reaction from any addressee. The predominance of this type can be observed not only in those cases where the verb is in first person singular, but also in third person singular (approximately in 89% of cases):

Aquella mujer era mi primera oportunidad, pero también podía ser la última. "¿Entenderá caste-llano?", me dije, tratando de descifrar el rostro de la muchacha que distraídamente, todavía sin verme, arrastraba por el camino sus polvorientas pantuflas de cuero.

That woman was my first chance, but she could also be the last one. "Does she understand-prob. Spanish?" I said to myself trying to learn something from the face of the girl who, still without seeing me, scuffed her dusty leather slippers on the path.

(ÚČNK – InterCorp. 10.08.2017. Gabriel García Márquez – *Relato de un náufrago*, the English translation is ours.)

—¿De dónde salió esta criatura? preguntaba masticando el aire. ¿Será mi hija, mi nieta o una alu-cinación de mi cerebro enfermo? Es morena, pero tiene los ojos parecidos a los míos... Ven aquí, chiquilla, para mirarte de cerca.

"Where did this child come from?" he asked himself, moving his law jaw. Is-prob. she my daughter, my granddaughter or a hallucination of my sick brain? Her skin is dark, but her eyes look like mine... Come here, kid, so I can take a closer look at you.

(ÚČNK – InterCorp. 10.08.2017. Isabel Allende – *Eva Luna*, the English translation is ours.)

In both cases, the *hablará* paradigm is used to emphasize the dubitative character of the question, the presence of the seme "probability" is, however, problematic. The function of this mood becomes even more apparent in those situations where an addressee is also present. Using the probabilitive, the speaker manifests the non-appellative character of his question where the MM potential prevails:

Entonces mi madre me dijo: "ah, dice Tere que vayas. Vino a buscarte." "¿Ah, sí?" le dije yo; "qué raro, ¿qué querrá?" Y de veras no sabía para qué me había buscado, era la primera vez que lo hacía y sospeché algo. Pero no lo que pasó. "Se ha enterado de mi cumpleaños y me va a felicitar", decía yo. Estuve en su casa de dos saltos.

And then my mother told me: "by the way, Tere says you should stop by. She came looking for you." "Oh, did she?" I replied; "that's strange, what does she want-prob.?" And I really didn't know why she had been looking for me, it was the first time she did it and I suspected something. But not the thing that actually happened. "She found out about my birthday and she is going to wish me well," I said to myself. I ran to her house.

(ÚČNK – InterCorp. 10.08.2017. Mario Vargas Llosa – *La ciudad y los perros*, the English translation is ours.)

The indicative in the same context would imply that the speaker expects a reply to his question. While the sequence ended with *¿qué querrá?* followed by an internal monologue does not seem unfinished, the use of the indicative would produce an expectation for a response, the reader would miss an answer.

We may generally conclude that in all the above-presented examples, the *hablará* paradigm feels more natural and its substitution with the indicative (however not impossible) would not be ideal. Its strong position in this type of utterances is also confirmed by the high overall frequency of the interpretation type A that is about 76%.[60]

6.2 CONCLUSION

We might state that the original presupposition that the probabilitive has a different role in interrogative sentences than in declarative ones has been confirmed. The corpus analysis has proven that it appears with a high frequency in non-appellative questions and its main role is to underline the dubitative character of the utterance. This translates into the fact that the other participants of the communication situation do not feel obliged to react to the question. The verbal mood is often the only distinctive feature that differentiates an appellative question from a non-appellative one (we could also consider the intonation in a spoken discourse).

This leads us to the conclusion that when combined with the MM interrogative, the probabilitive does not contain the seme of "probability," this being substituted by the seme "dubitation." We, therefore, propose the term *dubitative* for the use of the *hablará* paradigm in interrogative sentences and we characterize it as a morphological expression of the MM potential dubitative.

The fact that this modal meaning appears solely in interrogative utterances is yet another proof that modal meanings strongly affect each other. The relationship that has been analyzed in this chapter can be understood in two ways. We can observe that the MM interrogative influences the MM potential (more precisely its probabilitive subtype), changing some of its semantic components, suppressing the semes "probability" and "supposition" and strengthening the dubitation. We might also state that the presence of the dubitative changes the character of the question (more concretely, it changes the type of its volitional component) and it transports it from the framework of appellative questions to the framework of the non-appellative ones. This does not happen in every circumstance, this kind of mutual influence is, nevertheless, frequent in nowadays Spanish.

While it was not our original objective, the analyses have also proven the strong position of the probabilitive in Spanish. The polyfunctionality of the *hablará* paradigm inside the MMP is a proof of its full incorporation into the Spanish modal system and we may conclude that using this paradigm for expressing probability, supposition or dubitation cannot be considered figurative use of the future indicative in the nowadays language anymore. We consider, thus, terms such as epistemic future (*futuro epistémico*) or future of conjecture (*futuro de conjetura*) as inappropriate for Spanish.

---

60 However, we must bear in mind that the result might be to a certain level influenced by the type of text that form our corpus. Non-appellative questions appear generally more often in literature.

7. MODAL MEANING POTENTIAL →
MODAL MEANING VOLITIVE

We have already analysed both the MM potential and the MM volitive, concentrating on their relationship with the modal meanings evaluative and interrogative. Now we will study their mutual collaboration that has been mentioned only peripherally.

The MM volitive and the MM potential pervade each other in several areas. They have in common the seme of non-reality which defines the process presented in a proposition as possible, but not certain. When analysing predicates such as *desear* (*to wish*), *querer* (*to want*), *animar* (*to encourage*), *rogar* (*to beg*), *pedir* (*to ask for*), *exigir* (*to demand*), *conseguir* (*to achieve*), *permitir* (*to allow*), *lograr* (*to achieve*) and *obligar* (*to oblige*), Ahern (2008: 21) states that

> their meaning implies that the situation of the subordinate clause is presented as possible and, thus, prospective (i.e. referring to future) with respect to the reference tense of the main clause predicate. In other words, what all these predicates have in common is that they determine that the embedded clause is understood as a situation that is not fulfilled and that might be desirable or not.[61]

Yet, the strongest manifestation of the relationship between *p* and *v* is to be found in the semantics of Spanish modal verbs that will be analyzed on the following pages.

7.1 SPANISH MODAL VERBS

When speaking about the Spanish modals, Spanish grammars prefer the term *modal periphrases* (see, for example: Gómez Torrego 1999; RAE 2009). However, we will use Zavadil's terminology (see, for example, Zavadil 1980: 114–115) and we will follow the

---

61 Original quotation (the translation is ours): "su significado implica que la situación de la oración subordinada se presenta como posible, y por tanto prospectiva (es decir, referida al futuro) con respecto al tiempo de referencia del predicado subordinante. En otros términos, lo que comparten todos estos predicados consiste en el hecho de que determinan que la oración subordinada se entienda como una situación aún no realizada, que puede ser deseable o no."

term *modal verbs* that reflects better the way we understand these constructions (we are primarily interested in modal verbs as themselves, not in the periphrastic character of constructions they appear in).

There is no general accord regarding the number of modal verbs that can be found in Spanish. RAE (2009: 2140–2154) mentions primarily only *tener que*, *deber (de)*, *poder*, *haber que* and *haber de*. Their meanings could be summarised as follows:

1) *Tener que*
   Strong obligation resulting from an external source; low potentiality; closest to the English *have to*.
2) *Deber (de)*
   Medium degree of obligation resulting from moral or generally accepted rules; medium level of potentiality, comparable to the probabilitive; closest to the English *should*.
3) *Poder*
   Open possibility, closest to the English *can*.
4) *Haber que*
   Only used as impersonal, strong obligation, closest to the English *it is necessary that*.
5) *Haber de*
   Generally used in literary language, its meaning is similar to *tener que*.

Gómez Torrego (1999: 3362–3364) speaks also about other infinitive constructions collaborating in the expression of modality where he includes the verbs *lograr (to achieve)*, *conseguir (to achieve)*, *intentar (to try)*, *tratar (to try)* and *querer (to want)*. We will concentrate only on those verbs that under no circumstances permit the completion by a subordinate clause with the subjunctive. Further on, we exclude *haber que*, that appears only it the third person singular and is restricted to non-personal expressions, and *haber de* which is in many ways similar to *tener que* and differs, first and foremost, stylistically, not from the point of view of modality. We will, thus, focus on the modals *poder*, *deber (de)* and *tener que* that can behave as markers of both the MM potential and the MM volitive:

(1)   Puede estudiar. ≈ It is possible that he studies. // He is capable of studying. / He has a permission to study.
(2)   Debe (de) estudiar. ≈ He probably studies. / He has an obligation to study.
(3)   Tiene que estudiar. ≈ It is very probable that he studies. / He has an obligation to study.

Linguistic approaches to their analysis can be divided into various groups. We will now present the most important ones and always mention several linguistic works that we consider interesting inside the given group:

1) As we have already mentioned, constructions with these verbs are the object of study of linguists who analyse the issues related to the verbal periphrases in Spanish (e.g. Gómez Torrego 1999, García Fernández et al. 2006). However, these authors are primarily interested in the periphrastic character of these constructions and do not pay much attention to the place of modal verbs inside the whole modal system. This aspect is stressed only by Fernández de Castro (1999).
2) The second group is represented by authors who analyse the semantics of Spanish modals. These are often presented in contrast with the English modals and the authors focus on their uses in different contexts, presenting, thus, a typology of their possible interpretations. Interesting studies in this field have been presented by Sirbu-Dumitrescu (1988), Silva Corvalán (1995) or Cornillie (2007). We approached in a similar way the verb *poder* in Chapter 5.
3) Slightly less widely spread is the third possible approach that pays attention to the way the Spanish modals behave in different tenses. For this topic, see Laca (2006, 2010), Borgonovo – Cummins (2007).
4) For their role inside the modal system itself, Spanish modals are also mentioned by authors that study this area in its complexity (see Zavadil 1980, Haverkate 2002, Zavadil – Čermák 2010).

In this chapter, we present a synthesis of approaches 2 and 4. Given the primary focus of this book, we are especially interested in the factors that enable that the Spanish modals express both the MMV and the MMP.

This polyfunctionality is usually mentioned as one of the most important aspects of modal verbs and it is not limited only to Spanish modals. Similar phenomenon can be observed both in isolating languages (such as English) and inflected languages. In one of the most important works about Czech modality, Panevová – Benešová – Sgall (1971: 127) mention three meanings of the Czech modal *muset* (*have to*, *must*): necessity (*nutnostní*), possibility (*možnostní*) and will (*volní*). Nowadays Štícha (2013: 781–783) adds even two more possible meanings to the original three: need (*potřebnostní*) and probability (*pravděpodobnostní*).

Regarding the possible interpretations of Spanish modal verbs, RAE (2009: 2140) mentions root modality (*modalidad personal, radical*), that corresponds widely to the meanings of need, will and necessity, and epistemic modality (*modalidad epistémica, impersonal, proposicional*), that would correspond to the meanings of probability and possibility.

Zavadil – Čermák (2010: 264) introduce the Spanish modals in the following way:

> Clausal modal constructions are obligatory in Spanish for the so-called **modal verbs** (verbs with fully modal meaning): *querer* (MM volitive intentional), *tener que* (MM volitive of necessity – necessity is an objectively conceived will), *deber* (MM volitive of necessity), *haber de* (MM volitive of necessity) and *poder* (MM potential of possibility).[62]

---

62   Original quotation (the translation is ours): "Klauzární modální konstrukce jsou ve španělštině závazné pro tzv. **modální slovesa** (slovesa s čistě modálním významem): *querer* (MV volní intenční), *tener que* (MV volní

The definition of *deber* is further specified:

The modal verb *deber* 'to have an obligation' with the modal meaning volitive of necessity expresses, together with an infinitive, a **debetive notion**, but when used with the preposition *de*, it acquires the meaning **potential probabilitive**. However, this delimitation corresponds to the normative use of language. In practice, especially in the spoken language, both constructions can be interchanged freely (Zavadil – Čermák 2010: 266).[63]

We will take this terminology as a starting point, nevertheless, in order to achieve greater terminological precision, we will extend the list of subtypes of the MM volitive and the MM potential. For the interpretation that is called *modalidad radical* by RAE, we will use the terms MM volitive of necessity / of appropriateness / of possibility, for the epistemic interpretation (*modalidad epistémica*), the terms MM potential of necessity / probabilitive / of possibility.

7.2 RELATIONSHIP BETWEEN WILL AND POTENTIALITY

This relationship was already noted by Lyons (1986 [1977]: 832) who claims that "the notion of permission [...] is related to possibility in the same way that obligation is related to necessity." We can find a similar analogy between the MMV and the MMP with the modal verbs.

In their volitive interpretation, *tener que* and *deber* characterise the content of an utterance as more or less necessary, resulting either from an order or external circumstances (*tener que*), either from moral, ethics or general customs (*deber*). For a better distinction between these semantic notions, we prefer the terms MM volitive of necessity (*tener que*) and MM volitive of appropriateness (*deber*).

Like the level of indispensability (with the volitive interpretation), also the level of probability is lower with *deber* in comparison with *tener que* (in the potential interpretation). While *tener que* expresses a strong inference and conviction of the speaker that could be compared to the potential (or epistemic, in general terms) uses of the English modal *must*, *deber de* is very close to the probabilitive, expressing, thus, a medium level of certainty. For potential interpretations of *tener que*, we apply the term MM potential of necessity, for potential interpretations of *deber de*, we use the term MM potential probabilitive.

---

nutnostní – nutnost je objektivizovaná vůle), *deber* (MV volní nutnostní), *haber de* (MV volní nutnostní), *poder* (MV potenciální možnostní)."

63   Original quotation (the translation is ours): "Modální sloveso **deber** 'mít povinnost' s významem volním nutnostním vyjadřuje ve spojení s infinitivem významový **odstín debitivní**, je-li však užito předložky *de*, nabývá významu **potenciálního probabilitivního**. To je ovšem významové vymezení odpovídající normě spisovného jazyka. V praxi, zejména v jazyce mluveném, jsou obě konstrukce volně zaměňovány."

In a similar way, the level of volition / potentiality is expressed also by *poder* that can be found at the opposite side of the scale. In its volitive interpretation, it defines an event as theoretically possible with respect to the capabilities of the subject:

(4) Puedes conducir ≈ You can drive (You are capable of driving, you have a driver's licence),

or external circumstances:

(5) Puedes conducir ≈ You may drive (I give you my permission to drive, I lend you my car).

In neither case is the realization of the proposition presented in the dictum demanded by the speaker, he adopts a completely neutral posture. This translates into the possibility of completing these utterances by a sentence such as *si quieres* (*if you wish so*). Similar construction with *deber* or *tener que* would be practically impossible:

(6) Puedes conducir si quieres.
(7) ??Debes conducir si quieres.
(8) *Tienes que conducir si quieres.

With an utterance with *poder* (in the volitive interpretation), the speaker offers a possibility to the subject to do something, therefore, it is appropriate to use the term MM volitive of possibility.

The potential interpretation is again analogical to the volitive one. With *tener que* and *deber (de)* the speaker expresses his more (*tener que*) or less (*deber de*) firm conviction regarding the veracity of his proposition. *Poder* presents this proposition only as theoretically possible and the high level of potentiality enables the use of contra-factual completions that could not be used with other modals. A sequence such as *estar en la oficina* (*to be in the office*) introduced by *poder*, could be followed by *pero tal vez ya se ha ido* (*but he might have left already*), similar sentences introduced by *deber o tener que* would sound contradictory:

(9) Puede estar en la oficina, pero tal vez ya se ha ido.
(10) ??Debe de estar en la oficina, pero tal vez ya se ha ido.
(11) *Tiene que estar en la oficina, pero tal vez ya se ha ido.

The roots of the parallelism between the volitive and potential interpretation are very deep and can be found in the very substance of terms like *possibility*, *probability* or *necessity*. The situation is aptly described by Gómez Torrego (1999: 3348):

Each "probability" contains also an "obligation." When we say, for example, *Mi padre debe de estar en casa* [(*My father must be at home*)] (= "it is probable that he is..."), the speaker expresses a hypothesis obliged by external or pragmatic circumstances: because there is a light in the house; because it is already late; because we have heard some noise etc., i.e. there is a situation "cause" (the different sequences of *because*) that obliges that my father is at home.[64]

This can be also applied in the opposite way, i.e. every necessity or obligation, depending on how strong it is, leads to a higher or lower level of certainty that the event will take place. In its volitive interpretation, *Puedes conducir* presents the event of the dictum as theoretically permitted and, therefore, not sure. *Tienes que conducir* implies the necessity of realization which translates into a higher probability.

7.3 CONCLUSION

The seme "non-reality" that is shared by the MMV and the MMP links the two modal meanings on a basal level and enables their cooperation. The polyfunctionality of modal verbs is only an external manifestation of this relationship. This can be indirectly proven also by the interchangeability of *deber* and *deber de*. They should be, theoretically, markers of different MMs, yet, the interconnection of the MM volitive and the MM potential lead to their confusion. The relationship between the MMV and the MMP can be schematically represented as follows:

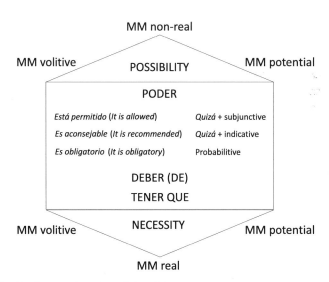

Image 9: Relationships between the MMV and the MMP

---

64   Original quotation (the translation is ours): "En toda 'probabilidad' se esconde una 'obligación'. Cuando se dice, por ejemplo, *Mi padre debe de estar en casa* (= 'es probable que esté...'), el hablante expresa una hipótesis obligado por las circunstancias externas o pragmáticas: porque hay luz en la casa; porque ya es tarde; porque se ha oído algún ruido, etc., es decir, se da una situación 'causa' (las distintas secuencias del *porque*) que obliga a que mi padre esté en casa."

The basis for both the modal meaning volitive and the modal meaning potential is at least a theoretical possibility of realization of the propositional content which is represented by *poder*. The scale continues through necessity (*deber – tener que*) that logically results into the MM real that characterizes a proposition as corresponding to reality. Spanish modals form the skeleton of this scale, however, since they formally behave as periphrastic verbal constructions and do not permit a closer modal differentiation of the verb in the dictum (that can appear only in the infinitive form), the possibility of further shading of the speaker's subjective posture is very limited here. This means that the modal verbs are an important part of Spanish modality, but they cannot be identified with it. At the cost of a certain simplification, we can assume that their importance is directly related to the amount of isolating features in a concrete language. It is by no way a coincidence that English disposes of a relatively wide spectrum of modal verbs that enable a further modulation of the speaker's attitude. At the same time, these verbs are used more often and in situations where Spanish can use a different modal resource, as shown in the following set of examples taken from the parallel corpus:

> I mean you <u>may think</u> it's a long way down the road to the chemist, but that's just peanuts to space.
> Quiero decir que <u>quizá piense-*subj.*</u> que es como un largo paseo por la calle hasta la farmacia, pero eso no es nada comparado con el espacio.
> (UČNK – InterCorp. 23.08.2017. Douglas Adams – *The Hitch Hiker's Guide to the Galaxy*, translator: Benito Gómez Ibáñez.)

> They <u>must have</u> Bernini references.
> <u>Habrá-*present prob.*</u> referencias a Bernini.
> (UČNK – InterCorp. 23.08.2017. Dan Brown – *The Da Vinci Code*, translator: Juanjo Estrella.)

> It was thought that you <u>might turn</u> far aside to avoid pursuit, and become lost in the Wilderness.
> Se decía que tu <u>harías-*past tense prob.*</u> un rodeo para evitar que te persiguieran y que te perderías en las tierras desiertas.
> (UČNK – InterCorp. 23.08.2017. J. R. R. Tolkien – *The Fellowship of the Ring*, translator: Luis Domenech.)

> I <u>could have gone</u> deeper if I'd known –
> <u>Hubiera ido-*pluperfect subj., substituting perfect cond.*</u> más a fondo, de haber sabido que…
> (UČNK – InterCorp. 23.08.2017. Francis Scott Fitzgerald – *The Great Gatsby*, translator: E. Piñas.)

Spanish, that maintains the fusional character of its verbal system, does not need such a vast range of uses of the modals and it can distinguish even very subtle modal differences by the combination of lexical means and verbal moods – the indicative, the subjunctive, the probabilitive and the conditional.

8. CONCLUSION

We have confirmed the initial assumption that the combination or blending of several modal meanings can be observed at all language levels and the problematics of the areas where different MMs meet cannot be considered marginal. On the contrary, concrete analyses presented in the previous chapters prove that these areas are a natural part of the modal system and their analysis proves to be useful, in some cases even essential, for a deeper understanding of Spanish modality.

Despite the fact that even at the very beginning we expected that there would be relatively many areas where different MMs meet, their number and, especially, the wide scale of ways in which MMs combined with each other exceeded our initial expectations. We have also encountered several contexts where there were even more than two MMs that combined or penetrated each other.

8.1 COMBINATIONS OF MMS

Ways of combining different MMs can be summarized into three basic types: scalar realization, confluence of MMs and blending of MMs in their basis.

8.1.1 SCALAR REALIZATION

This type was mentioned in Chapter 2 that analysed the relationship between the MM real and the MM potential. We have observed that this relationship can be considered unique inside the Spanish modality, for there is no accumulation of two MMs, but their gradual transformation. This transformation has several phases that translate into a wide spectrum of partially synonymous expressions of potentiality / reality that can be followed (in some circumstances) by the congruential subjunctive.

The alternation between the indicative and the subjunctive in order to differentiate subtle semantic nuances is a tool of moving on the scale that has no direct counterpart in languages such as English. The scalar realization is different also in Romance languages, compare, for example, the Italian that uses the conjunctive in a different way:

Spanish: *Creo que es; Quizás es / sea* (*I believe it is*-ind.); (*Maybe it is*-ind. / subj.)
Italian: *Credo che sia / è; Forse è* (*I believe it is*-subj. / ind.[65]); (*Maybe it is*-ind.)

We can, thus, observe that the scale is organized differently even in related languages.

Analyses in Chapter 2 also suggest that the perception of this scale depends to a certain extent on the idiolect of a concrete speaker (we have seen that different authors often used a different mood in similar contexts). This leads us again to the conclusion that modality is an extremely complex area that is susceptible to the subjective attitude of speakers. It, therefore, appears to be essential to understand the language modality as an area relatively independent on the modal logic and it is useful to create individual theoretical models of this area for each language separately.

8.1.2 CONFLUENCE OF MMS

The most thorough analysis of this type was presented in Chapter 3 that analysed the contexts where the MM potential and the MM evaluative appeared simultaneously. In the context of the other studies, this relationship proved to be the less common one. The confluence of these two MMs can be observed only in constructions introduced by concrete verbs, we concentrated on the verbs *esperar* (*to hope, to expect*) and *temer(se)* (*to be afraid*), we might eventually consider also verbs such as *confiar* (*to trust*) or *comprender* (*to understand*), *entender* (*to understand*), we have also mentioned the constructions with *es probable / possible que* (*it is probable / possible that*) and *no dudo (de) que* (*I don't doubt that*). In general, it is nevertheless possible to state that the MMP and the MME behave as relatively independent. We also mentioned some other examples of this type of relationship with *admitir* (*to admit*) and *aceptar* (*to accept*), nevertheless, we focused our attention on less isolated manifestations of relationships among MMs.

This type differs fundamentally from the scalar representation, since the semes belonging to each MM appear simultaneously in one utterance. We have also seen that their occurrence within one sentence cannot be understood as mere coexistence where two MM appear together and do not react to the presence of the other one. Our analyses have shown that the semes "evaluation" and "potentiality" can cooperate mutually. This cooperation is formally manifested by the subjunctive that appears in the dictum. This modal congruence has proven to be systemic, i.e. the subjunctive clearly prevailed in all analysed constructions and its eventual absence could be justified by weakening of one of the two MMs.

This observation may seem surprising, especially if we bear in mind that, as stated above, this relationship is the less distinct one inside the Spanish modality and the contexts for its occurrence are limited. The fact that even here modality reacts system-

---

65   The subjunctive (conjunctive) is the most common option in this type of constructions.

atically to a co-occurrence of two MMs is another proof that areas where several MMs meet are completely natural in the language, function as its solid part and that Spanish manifests a high degree of modal sensibility for them.

8.1.3 BLENDING OF MMS IN THEIR BASIS

This kind of relationship was found most often. In the Chapters 4, 5, 6 and 7, we analysed from several points of view questions related to MMs volitive and interrogative that proved to be strongly dependent not only on each other (the volitive component is an inherent part of the MMI), but also on other MMs. One of the semantic components of the MM volitive is the seme "potentiality" (i.e. uncertainty regarding the realization of a process) and "evaluation" that relates to the process that is presented as a subject of speaker's will. Potentiality is also included (together with the seme "volition," i.e. a petition for a piece of information) in the MM interrogative (the process that is subjected to question cannot be presented as certain).

Such frequent (and, again, completely natural) concurrence of MMs even in the very basis of some of them proves once again that analysed areas of combinations of modal meanings are not fields of tension or strain inside the Spanish modality, they are not a priori problematic areas that language tries to balance. On the contrary, very often they are essential for its functioning, it is impossible to ask a question without its volitive element (not even in the case of rhetorical questions, see Chapter 6) and a speaker cannot express his will without the simultaneous evaluation of the eventual event (see Chapter 4).

8.2 SUMMARY

Conclusions drawn in this chapter lead to one rather surprising observation. When analysing the Spanish modality from the perspective of combinations of modal meanings, we found only three MMs that do not contain semes related to other MMs in their basis: the MM potential, the MM real and the MM evaluative.

The strong position of MMs potential and real inside the Spanish modality was expected, since the status of speaker's (un)certainty (or the epistemic modality) is usually not questioned in works about modality. We may recall Chapter 1 where different approaches to modality where presented. While the expressions of will / necessity are understood differently by different authors, the understanding of epistemic modality as one of the pillars of modality in general is, in principle, unanimous.

However, analyses presented in this study point out that another basic MM in Spanish is the MM evaluative that is in many theoretical concepts put aside (in the Slavonic linguistics, for example, emotionality is often not seen as modal at all). The situation in Spanish gives us many reasons to see this area as a modal one (the use of the subjunctive in utterances with the MME) and our observations lead us to the conclusion that the status of this MM inside the Spanish modal system is not only undoubtable, but even more important than it is generally thought. We can, therefore, conclude once more that a universal concept that in its basis operates only with the opposition epistemic – deontic (dynamic, root) modality is not always sufficient for a complex description of the Spanish modality.

As a follow-up to all that was stated above, we understand Spanish modality as a specific and extremely complex area that cannot be fully described with universal typology. Of course, we do not insinuate that precisely Spanish modality is somehow exceptional in comparison with modalities in other languages, we consider specific and relatively independent the modality of any language.

We consider the areas where different MMs meet inherent parts of the Spanish modal system. We have also encountered many contexts where we could observe the co-appearance of not only two, but even three MMs. It is a question for the future whether this number can be considered final or whether there are contexts that enable mutual influencing of four or even more MMs. We believe that an analysis of these areas (that have not been studied systematically yet) might shed some more light on our understanding of the Spanish (or any other) modal system.

BIBLIOGRAPHY

ACHARD, Michel. 2000. Selección de modo en construcciones oracionales de complemento. *Revista Española de Lingüística Aplicada*, volumen monográfico, pp. 153–173.

AHERN, Aoife. 2008. *El subjuntivo: contextos y efectos*. Madrid: Arco Libros.

ARCE CASTILLO, Ángela. 1998. Los conectores pragmáticos como índices de modalidad en español actual. *E. L. U. A.* 12, pp. 9–23.

AUROVÁ, Miroslava. 2013. El uso del subjuntivo/indicativo con el operador de modalidad *quizá(s)*: Análisis del corpus. *Écho des études romanes* 9/1, pp. 19–33.

BALLY, Charles. 1965. *Linguistique générale et linguistique française*. Bern: Éditions France Berne.

BARRIOS SABADOR, María José. 2015. Variability in oral discourse: the case of *seguramente*. A comparative analysis with *quizá[s]* and *a lo mejor*. *Verba Hispanica* XXIII, pp. 61–86.

BARRIOS SABADOR, María José. 2016. Uso de indicativo y subjuntivo en los adverbios de modalidad epistémica de incertidumbre. Estudio en un corpus informatizado. *E-AESLA 2*, pp. 260–273.

BIBER, Douglas et al. 1999. *Longman Grammar of Spoken and Written English*. London: Longman.

BLÜHDORN, Hardarik – REICHMANN, Tinka. 2010. Modal readings of sentence connectives in German and Portuguese. In M. G. Becker – E.-M. Remberger (eds.) *Modality and Mood in Romance: Modal interpretation, mood selection, and mood alternation*. Berlin: De Gruyter, pp. 15–38.

BORGONOVO, Claudia – CUMMINS, Sarah. 2007. Tensed modals. In L. Eguren – O. Fernandez Soriano (eds.) *Coreference, Modality, and Focus*. Amsterdam – Philadelphia: John Benjamins Publishing Company, pp. 1–18.

BRENNER, Katja. 2009. Formas de modalización del español. El superlativo absoluto con sufijo -*ísimo*. In G. Hassler – G. Volkmann (eds.) *Deixis y modalidad en textos narrativos*. Münster: Nodus Publikationen, pp. 153–164.

BYBEE, Joan – PERKINS, Revere – PAGLIUCA, William. 1994. *The Evolution of Grammar: Tense, aspect, and modality in the languages of the world*. Chicago – London: University of Chicago Press.

COATES, Jennifer. 1983. *The Semantics of the Modal Auxiliaries*. London: Croon Helm.

CORNILLIE, Bert. 2007. *Evidentiality and Epistemic Modality in Spanish (Semi)Auxiliaries: A cognitive-functional approach*. Berlin – New York: Mouton de Gruyter.

ČERMÁK, František – ROSEN, Alexandr. 2012. The case of InterCorp, a multilingual parallel corpus. *International Journal of Corpus Linguistics* vol. 13, no. 3, pp. 411–427.

ČERMÁK, Petr – VAVŘÍN, Martin. 2016. *Korpus InterCorp – Spanish, version 9 from 9. 9. 2016*. Ústav Českého národního korpusu FF UK, Praha. [online]. Retrieved from: <http://www.korpus.cz>.

DECLERCK, Renaat. 2011. The definition of modality. In A. Patard – F. Brisard (eds.) *Cognitive Approaches to Tense, Aspect, and Epistemic Modality*. Amsterdam – Philadelphia: John Benjamins Publishing Company, pp. 21–44.

DUMITRESCU, Domnița. 1993. Función pragma-discursiva de la interrogación ecoica usada como respuesta en español. In H. Haverkate – K. Hengeveld – G. Mulder (eds.) *Aproximaciones pragmalingüísticas al español.* Amsterdam: Rodopi, pp. 51–85.

FERNÁNDEZ DE CASTRO, Félix. 1999. *Las perífrasis verbales en el español actual.* Madrid: Gredos.

FRANZ, Annika. 2009. ¿Modalización mediante la deixis personal? Un análisis del uso de yo y tú en diálogos de novelas. In G. Hassler – G. Volkmann (eds.) *Deixis y modalidad en textos narrativos.* Münster: Nodus Publikationen, pp. 107–122.

GARCÍA FERNÁNDEZ, Luis et al. 2009. *Diccionario de perífrasis verbales.* Madrid: Gredos.

GÓMEZ TORREGO, Leonardo. 1999. Los verbos auxiliares. Las perífrasis verbales de infinitivo. In I. Bosque – V. Demonte (eds.) *Gramática descriptiva de la lengua española.* Madrid: Espasa Calpe, pp. 3323–3389.

GONZÁLEZ VÁZQUEZ, Mercedes. 2002. Hacia un concepto de modalidad. *Linguistica Pragensia* 12/2, pp. 57–82.

GRANDE ALIJA, Francisco. 2002. *Aproximación a las modalidades enunciativas.* León: Universidad de León, Secretariado de Publicaciones y Medios Audiovisuales.

GUITART, Jorge. 1990. Aspectos pragmáticos del modo en los complementos de predicados de conocimiento y de adquisición de conocimiento en español. In I. Bosque (ed.) *Indicativo y subjuntivo.* Madrid: Taurus, pp. 315–329.

HAVERKATE, Henk. 1979. *Impositive Sentences in Spanish: Theory and description in linguistic pragmatics.* Amsetrdam: North-Holland Publishing Company, 1979.

HAVERKATE, Henk. 2002. *The Syntax, Semantics and Pragmatics of Spanish Mood.* Philadelphia: John Benjamins Publishing Company.

HENGEVELD, Kees. 1988. Illocution, mood and modality in a functional grammar of Spanish. *Journal of Semantics* 6, pp. 227–269.

HUMMEL, Martin. 2004. *El valor básico del subjuntivo español y románico.* Cáceres: Universidad de Extremadura.

JIMÉNEZ JULIÁ, Tomás. 1989. Modalidad, modo verbal y *modus* clausal en español. *Verba. Anuario galego de filoloxía* 16, pp. 175–214.

KANASUGI, Petra. 2013. *Vývoj od tvaru* -m.u *k tvarům* -ó/-jó *a daró jako příklad gramatikalizace a subjektivizace.* Doctoral dissertation, Praha: Charles University.

KLÉGR, Aleš – KUBÁNEK, Michal – MALÁ, Markéta – ROHRAUER, Leona – ŠALDOVÁ, Pavlína – VAVŘÍN, Martin. 2016. *Corpus InterCorp – English, version 9 from 9. 9. 2016.* Ústav Českého národního korpusu FF UK, Praha. [online]. Retreived from: <http://www.korpus.cz>.

KLÍMOVÁ, Eva. 2009. *Otázky vztahu slovesného modu a modality v italštině (na pozadí angličtiny a češtiny).* Opava: Slezská univerzita v Opavě.

KOVACCI, Ofelia. 1992. *Comentario gramatical: Teoría y práctica, II.* Madrid: Arco Libros, 1992.

KRATOCHVÍLOVÁ, Dana. 2013a. Selección de modo indicativo o subjuntivo con adverbios como *quizá(s), tal vez, posiblemente y probablemente. Romanistica Pragensia* 19, pp. 137–148.

KRATOCHVÍLOVÁ, Dana. 2013b. Las relaciones entre el significado modal real y el significado modal potencial en español. *Linguistica Pragensia* 23/2, pp. 73–83.

KRATOCHVÍLOVÁ, Dana. 2014. Univerzální koncepce modality a její aplikace na španělský modální systém. *Časopis pro moderní filologii* 96/1, pp. 58–73.

KRATOCHVÍLOVÁ, Dana. 2016. El subjuntivo español como tema central de investigación. *Acta Universitatis Carolinae Philologica* 3, pp. 197–209.

KRATZER, Angelika. 1991. Modality. In Arnim von Stechow – Dieter Wunderlich (eds.) *Semantics: An international handbook of contemporary research.* Berlin: Walter de Gruyter, pp. 639–650.

LACA, Brenda. 2006. Tiempo, aspecto y la interpretación de los verbos modales en español. *Lingüística ALFAL* 17, pp. 9–44.

LACA, Brenda. 2010. Temporalidad y modalidad. In M. Casas Gómez (ed.) *Actas de las Jornadas de Lingüística 2006.* Cádiz: Publicaciones de la universidad de Cádiz, pp. 109–136.

LANGACKER, Ronald W. 1991a. *Foundations od Cognitive Grammar I. – Theoretical Prerequisites.* Stanford: Stanford University Press.

LANGACKER, Ronald. 1991b. *Foundations of Cognitive Grammar II. – Descriptive Application.* Stanford: Stanford University Press.

LANGACKER, Ronald. 2003. Extreme subjectification: English tense and modals. In H. Cuyckens – T. Berg – R. Dirven – K-U. Panther (eds.) *Motivation in Language: Studies in Honor of Günter Radden.* Amsterdam: John Benjamins, pp. 3–26.

LYONS, John. 1986. *Semantics.* 2 vols. Cambridge: Cambridge University Press.

MALDONADO, Ricardo. 1995. Middle-Subjunctive Links. In P. Hashemipour – R. Maldonado – M. van Naerssen (eds.) *Studies in Language Learning and Spanish Linguistics in Honour of Tracy D. Terrell.* New York: McGraw Hill, pp. 399–418.

MATTE BON, Francisco. 1998. Gramática, pragmática y enseñanza comunicativa del español como lengua extranjera. *Carabela* 43, pp. 53–79.

MATTE BON, Franscisco. 2005a. *Gramática Comunicativa del español: De la idea a la lengua. Tomo I.* Madrid: Edelsa.

MATTE BON, Franscisco. 2005b. *Gramática Comunicativa del español: De la lengua a la idea. Tomo II.* Madrid: Edelsa.

MATTE BON, Francisco. 2008. El subjuntivo español como operador metalingüístico de gestión de información. *Revista de Didáctica ELE* 6/2008. [online]. Retrieved on 01.05.2017 from: <http://marcoele.com/el-subjuntivo-espanol-como-operador-metalinguistico-de-gestion-de-la-informacion/>.

MULDER, Gijs. 1993. ¿Por qué no coges el teléfono?: acerca de los actos de habla indirectos. In H. Haverkate – K. Hengeveld – G. Mulder (eds.) *Aproximaciones pragmalingüísticas al español.* Amsterdam: Rodopi, pp. 181–207.

NÁDVORNÍKOVÁ, Olga. 2016. *Le corpus multilingue InterCorp et les possibilités de son exploitation.* In D. Trotter – A. Bozzi – C. Fairon (eds.) *Actes du XXVIIe Congrès international de linguistique et de philologie romanes (Nancy, 15–20 juillet 2013). Section 16 : Projets en cours ; ressources et outils nouveaux.* Nancy: ATILF, pp. 223–237.

NÁDVORNÍKOVÁ, Olga. 2017. Pièges méthodologiques des corpus parallèles et comment les éviter. *Corela – cognition, représentation, langages* 15, pp. 1–28.

NORDSTRÖM, Jackie. 2010. *Modality and Subordinators.* Amsterdam – Philadelphia: John Benjamins Publishing Company.

NOWIKOW, Wiaczesław. 2001. *La alternancia de los modos Indicativo y Subjuntivo en las cláusulas subordinadas sustantivas: (metodología del análisis lingüístico).* Poznań: Wydawnictwo Naukowe Uniwersytetu Im. Adama Mickiewicza.

OTAOLA OLANO, Concepción. 1988. La modalidad (con especial referencia a la lengua española). *Revista de Filología Española* 68/1, pp. 97–117.

PALMER, Frank Robert. 1986. *Mood and Modality.* Cambridge: Cambridge University Press.

PALMER, Frank Robert. 2001. *Mood and Modality. Second edition.* Cambridge: Cambridge University Press.

PAMIES BERTRÁN, Antonio – VALEŠ, Miroslav. 2015. *El subjuntivo español y su equivalencia en checo.* Granada: Granada Lingvistica.

PANEVOVÁ, Jarmila – BENEŠOVÁ, Eva – SGALL, Petr. 1971. *Čas a modalita v češtině.* Praha: Univerzita Karlova.

PÉREZ SEDEÑO, María Encarnación. 2001. Subjetividad y modalidad lingüística. *EPOS* 15, pp. 57–70.

PORTNER, Paul. 2009. *Modality.* Oxford: Oxford University Press.

PORTO DAPENA, José Álvaro. 1991. *Del indicativo al subjuntivo: valores y usos de los modos del verbo.* Madrid: Arco Libros.

PORTOLÉS, José. 2004. *Pragmática para hispanistas.* Madrid: Editorial Síntesis.

RAE. 2009. *Nueva gramática de la lengua española.* Madrid: Espasa Libros.

RAE: Banco de datos (CREA). *Corpus de referencia del español actual.* [online]. Retrieved from: <http://www.rae.es>.

RAE: Banco de datos (CORPES XXI, v.. 0.82). *Corpus del Español del Siglo XXI.* [online]. Retrieved from: <http://www.rae.es>.

RESCHER, Nicolas. 1968. *Topics in Philosophical Logic.* Dortrecht: Reidel.

RIDRUEJO, Emilio. 1999. Modo y modalidad. El modo en las subordinadas sustantivas. In I. Bosque – V. Demonte (eds.) *Gramática descriptiva de la lengua española*. Madrid: Espasa Calpe, pp. 3209–3251.

RUBINSTEIN, Aynat. 2012. *Roots of Modality*. Doctoral dissertation, Amherst: University of Massachusetts.

RUIZ CAMPILLO, José Plácido. 2004. El subjuntivo es lógico: una actividad de concienciación. *redELE*, vol. 1.

RUIZ CAMPILLO, José Plácido. 2006. El concepto de no-declaración como valor del subjuntivo. Protocolo de instrucción operativa de la selección modal en español. In C. Pastor (ed.) *Actas del programa de formación para profesorado de ELE del Instituto Cervantes de Múnich*. München: Instituto Cervantes, pp. 1–51.

RUIZ CAMPILLO, José Plácido. 2008. El valor central del subjuntivo: ¿Informatividad o declaratividad?. *marcoELE*, vol. 7, pp. 1–44.

SASTRE RUANO, María Ángeles. 1997. *El subjuntivo en español*. Salamanca: Colegio de España.

SILVA-CORVALÁN, Carmen. 1995. Contextual conditions for the interpretation of 'poder' and 'deber' in Spanish. In J. Bybee – S. Fleischman (eds.) *Modality in Grammar and Discourse*. Amsterdam: Benjamins, pp. 67–105.

SIRBU-DUMITRESCU, Domniţa. 1988. Contribución al estudio de la semántica de los verbos modales en español (con ejemplos del habla de Madrid). *Hispania* 71/1, pp. 139–147.

SWEETSER, Eve. 1991. *From Etymology to Pragmatics: Metaphorical and cultural aspects of semantic structure*. Cambridge – New York – Melbourne: Cambridge University Press.

ŠTÍCHA, František et al. 2013. *Akademická gramatika spisovné češtiny*. Praha: Academia.

TRAUGOTT, Elizabeth. 2007. (Inter)subjectification and unidirectionality. *Journal of Historical Pragmatics* 8: 2, pp. 295–309.

TRAUGOTT, Elizabeth. 2011. (Inter)subjectivity and (inter)subjectification: A reassessment. In K. Davidse – L. Vandelanotte – H. Cuyckens (eds.) *Subjectification, Intersubjectification and Grammaticalization*. Berlin: Walter de Gruyter.

VEIGA, Alexandre. 1991. *Condicionales, concesivas y modo verbal en español*. Santiago de Compostela: Universidad de Santiago de Compostela.

VESTERINEN, Rainer. 2014. Extending the dominion of effective control – Its applicability to mood choice in Spanish and Portuguese. *Cognitive Linguistics* 25 (4), pp. 583–616.

VESTERINEN, Rainer – BYLUND, Emanuel. 2013. Towards a unified account of the Spanish subjunctive mood: Epistemic dominion and dominion of effective control. *Lingua* 131, pp. 179–198.

WASA, Atsuko. 1999. El subjuntivo y la modalidad. *Hispania* 82/1, pp. 121–127.

WASA, Atsuko. 2002. *A lo mejor* y el subjuntivo. *Hispania* 85/1, pp. 131–136.

YANOVICH, Igor. 2014. Symbouletic Modality. *Empiricial Issues in Syntax and Semantics* 10, pp. 161–178.

ZAVADIL, Bohumil. 1968. Medios expresivos de la categoría de modalidad en español. *Ibero-Americana Pragensia* 2, pp. 57–86.

ZAVADIL, Bohumil. 1975. Ensayo de una interpretación funcional de los modos españoles. *Romanistica Pragensia* 9, pp. 143–177.

ZAVADIL, Bohumil. 1979a. La delimitación de la categoría de modalidad. *Ibero-Americana Pragensia* 12, pp. 51–88.

ZAVADIL, Bohumil. 1979b. Sobre algunos aspectos dinámicos del sistema modal castellano. *Romanistica Pragensia* 12, pp. 109–116.

ZAVADIL, Bohumil. 1980. *Kategorie modality ve španělštině*. Praha: Univerzita Karlova.

ZAVADIL, Bohumil. 1995. *Současný španělský jazyk, II. Základní slovní druhy: slovesa*. Praha: Karolinum.

ZAVADIL, Bohumil. in press. *Mluvnice katalánštiny*. Quoted from manuscript.

ZAVADIL, Bohumil – ČERMÁK, Petr. 2008. *Sintaxis del español actual*. Praha: Karolinum.

ZAVADIL, Bohumil – ČERMÁK, Petr. 2010. *Mluvnice současné španělštiny*. Praha: Karolinum.

APPENDIX 1

LIST OF BOOKS INCLUDED IN THE SPANISH SUBCORPUS

Isabel Allende, *El bosque de los pigmeos*
Isabel Allende, *El reino del Dragón de Oro*
Isabel Allende, *El Zorro*
Isabel Allende, *Eva Luna*
Isabel Allende, *Hija de la fortuna*
Isabel Allende, *Inés del alma mía*
Isabel Allende, *La casa de los espíritus*
Isabel Allende, *La ciudad de las bestias*
Isabel Allende, *Paula*
Isabel Allende, *Retrato en sepia*
Pedro Almodóvar, *Patty Diphusa y otros textos*
Pedro Almodóvar, *Todo sobre mi madre*
Federico Andahazi, *El secreto de los flamencos*
Reinaldo Arenas, *El portero*
Guillermo Arriaga, *Amores perros*
Gustavo Adolfo Bécquer, *Leyendas*
(texts included in the Czech anthology *Hora duchů*, Prague: Vyšehrad, 1999.)
Mario Benedetti, *Buzón de tiempo*
Mario Benedetti, *Gracias por el fuego*
Mario Benedetti, *La borra del café*
Mario Benedetti, *La tregua*
Adolfo Bioy Casares, *La invención de Morel*
Adolfo Bioy Casares, *Plan de evasión*
Roberto Bolaño, *2666*
Roberto Bolaño, *El Tercer Reich*
Roberto Bolaño, *La literatura nazi en América*
Roberto Bolaño, *Los detectives salvajes*
Roberto Bolaño, *Nocturno de Chile*
Jorge Luis Borges, *El informe de Brodi*
Jorge Luis Borges, *Ficciones, El Aleph*
(texts included in the Czech anthology *Artefakty*, Prague: Odeon, 1969.)
Jorge Luis Borges, *Historia universal de la infamia*
Jorge Bucay, Silvia Salinas, *Amarse con los ojos abiertos*
Alejo Carpentier, *Concierto barroco*

Alejo Carpentier, *El arpa y la sombra*
Alejo Carpentier, *El reino de este mundo*
Alejo Carpentier, *El siglo de las luces*
Alejo Carpentier, *Los pasos perdidos*
Camilo José Cela, *La colmena*
Camilo José Cela, *La familia de Pascual Duarte*
Javier Cercas, *Soldados de Salamina*
Daína Chaviano, *El hombre, la hembra y el hambre*
Francisco Coloane, *Tierra de fuego*
Julio Cortázar, *Alguien que anda por ahí*
Julio Cortázar, *Final del juego*
Julio Cortázar, *Historias de cronopios y famas*
Julio Cortázar, *Los premios*
Julio Cortázar, *Rayuela*
Julio Cortázar, *Un tal Lucas*
Álvaro Cunqueiro, *Un hombre que se parecía a Orestes*
Miguel Delibes, *Cinco horas con Mario*
Miguel Delibes, *Diario de un cazador*
Miguel Delibes, *Los santos inocentes*
Lucía Etxebarría, *Amor, curiosidad, prozac y dudas*
Lucía Etxebarría, *Beatriz y los cuerpos celestes*
Carlos Fuentes, *Diana o La cazadora solitaria*
Carlos Fuentes, *Gringo viejo*
Carlos Fuentes, *La muerte de Artemio Cruz*
Carlos Fuentes, *Vlad*
Gabriel García Márquez, *Cien años de soledad*
Gabriel García Márquez, *Crónica de una muerte anunciada*
Gabriel García Márquez, *Del amor y otros demonios*
Gabriel García Márquez, *Doce cuentos peregrinos*
Gabriel García Márquez, *El amor en los tiempos del cólera*
Gabriel García Márquez, *El coronel no tiene quien le escriba*
Gabriel García Márquez, *El general en su laberinto*
Gabriel García Márquez, *El otoño del patriarca*
Gabriel García Márquez, *La aventura de Miguel Littín, clandestino en Chile.*
Gabriel García Márquez, *La hojarasca*
Gabriel García Márquez, *La increíble y triste historia de la cándida Eréndira y de su abuela desalmada*
Gabriel García Márquez, *La mala hora*
Gabriel García Márquez, *Los funerales de la Mamá Grande*
Gabriel García Márquez, *Memoria de mis putas tristes*
Gabriel García Márquez, *Noticia de un secuestro*
Gabriel García Márquez, *Relato de un náufrago*
Gabriel García Márquez, *Vivir para contarla*
Pedro Juan Gutiérrez, *El rey de La Habana*
José Jiménez Lozano, *El mudejarillo*
Carmen Laforet, *Nada*
Julio Llamazares, *La lluvia amarilla*
Javier Marías, *Corazón tan blanco*
Javier Marías, *Mañana en la batalla piensa en mí*
Javier Marías, *Salvajes y sentimentales*
Javier Marías, *Todas las almas*
Juan Marsé, *Caligrafía de los sueños*
Juan Marsé, *La muchacha de las bragas de oro*
Juan Marsé, *Rabos de lagartija*

Luis Martín-Santos, *Tiempo de silencio*
Eduardo Mendoza, *El asombroso viaje de Pomponio Flato*
Eduardo Mendoza, *La verdad sobre el caso Savolta*
Mayra Montero, *Como un mensajero tuyo*
Mayra Montero, *Última noche que pasé contigo*
Javier Moro, *El sari rojo*
Javier Moro, *Pasión india*
Julia Navarro, *La hermandad de la Sábana Santa*
Juan Carlos Onetti, *Para una tumba sin nombre, Tan triste como ella y otros cuentos*
(texts included in the Czech anthology *Bezejmenný hrob a jiné příběhy*, Prague: Mladá fronta, 1987.)
José Ortega y Gasset, *La rebelión de las masas*
Arturo Pérez-Reverte, *El club Dumas*
Arturo Pérez-Reverte, *El maestro de esgrima*
Arturo Pérez-Reverte, *La carta esférica*
Arturo Pérez-Reverte, *La piel del tambor*
Arturo Pérez-Reverte, *La reina del sur*
Arturo Pérez-Reverte, *La tabla de Flandes*
Horacio Quiroga, *Cuentos*
(texts included in the Czech anthology *Návrat anakondy*. Prague: Odeon, 1978.)
Augusto Roa Bastos, *Yo, el supremo*
Juan Rulfo, *Llano en llamas. Pedro Páramo*
Ernesto Sabato, *Abbadón el exterminador*
Ernesto Sabato, *El túnel*
Eduardo Sacheri, *La pregunta de sus ojos*
Natalia Sanmartín Fenollera, *El despertar de la señorita Prim*
Luis Sepúlveda, *La sombra de lo que fuimos*
Luis Sepúlveda, *Un viejo que leía novelas de amor*
Javier Sierra, *El secreto egipcio de Napoleón*
Javier Sierra, *La cena secreta*
Lorenzo Silva, *La flaqueza del bolchevique*
Maruja Torres, *Mientras vivimos*
Pablo Tusset, *Lo mejor que le puede pasar a un cruasán*
Miguel de Unamuno, *Abel Sánchez*
Miguel de Unamuno, *Nada menos que todo un hombre*
Miguel de Unamuno, *Niebla*
Miguel de Unamuno, *San Manuel Bueno, mártir*
Zoe Valdés, *La nada cotidiana*
Mario Vargas Llosa, *El hablador*
Mario Vargas Llosa, *El paraíso en la otra esquina*
Mario Vargas Llosa, *El sueño del celta*
Mario Vargas Llosa, *Guerra del fin del mundo*
Mario Vargas Llosa, *La casa verde*
Mario Vargas Llosa, *La ciudad y los perros*
Mario Vargas Llosa, *La Fiesta del Chivo*
Mario Vargas Llosa, *La guerra del fin del mundo*
Mario Vargas Llosa, *La tía Julia y el escribidor*
Mario Vargas Llosa, *Lituma en los Andes*
Mario Vargas Llosa, *Pantaleón y las visitadoras*
Mario Vargas Llosa, *¿Quién mató a Palomino Molero?*
Mario Vargas Llosa, *Travesuras de la niña mala*
Enrique Vila Matas, *Bartleby y compañía*
Jorge Zúñiga Pavlov, *La Casa Blú. Historias del bajomundo latinoamericano*
Jorge Zúñiga Pavlov, *Mudanzas y otros movimientos*

Appendix 2

List of books included in the English-Spanish subcorpus

Douglas Adams, *So Long, and Thanks for All the Fish*
(*Hasta luego y gracias por el pescado*, transl. Benito Gómez Ibáñez)
Douglas Adams, *The Hitch Hiker's Guide to the Galaxy*
(*Guía del autoestopista galáctico*, transl. Benito Gómez Ibáñez)
Douglas Adams, *The Restaurant at the End of the Universe*
(*El restaurante del fin del mundo*, transl. Benito Gómez Ibáñez)
Dan Brown, *Angels and Demons*
(*Ángeles y demonios*, transl. Eduardo G. Murillo)
Dan Brown, *The Da Vinci Code*
(*El código Da Vinci*, transl. Juanjo Estrella)
Lewis Carroll, *Alice in Wonderland*
(*Alicia en el País de las Maravillas*, transl. Ramón Buckley)
Nicholas Evans, *The Divide*
(*Cuando el abismo separa*, transl. Ignacio Gómez Calvo)
Francis Scott Fitzgerald, *The Great Gatsby*
(*El gran Gatsby*, transl. E. Piñas)
Erich Fromm, *To Have or to Be?*
(*¿Tener o ser?*, transl. Carlos Valdés)
John Grisham, *The Partner*
(*El socio*, transl. Mercè López)
Stephen Hawking, *A Brief History of Time: From the Big Bang to Black Holes*
(*Historia del tiempo: del Big Bang a los agujeros negros*, transl. Miguel Ortuño)
Kazuo Ishiguro, *An Artist of the Floating World*
(*Un artista del mundo flotante*, transl. Ángel Luis Hernández Francés)
Stephen King, *Carrie*
(*Carrie*, transl. Gregorio Vlastelica)
James Lovelock, *The Ages of Gaia: A Biography of Our Living Earth*
(*Las edades de Gaia. Una biografía de nuestro planeta vivo*, transl. Joan Grimalt)
Ian McEwan, *Atonement*
(*Expiación*, transl. Jaime Zulaika)
Barack Obama, *Inaugural Address*
(*Discurso inaugural del presidente*, transl. María Luisa Rodríguez Tapia)
George Orwell, *1984*
(*1984*, transl. Rafael Vázquez Zamora)

George Orwell, *Animal Farm*
(*La rebelión en la granja*, transl. Rafael Abella)
Philip Roth, *The Human Stain*
(*La mancha humana*, transl. Jordi Fibla)
J. K. Rowling, *Harry Potter and the Chamber of Secrets*
(*Harry Potter y la cámara secreta*, transl. Adolfo Muñoz García, Nieves Martín Azofra)
J. K. Rowling, *Harry Potter and the Deathly Hallows*
(*Harry Potter y las Reliquias de la Muerte*, transl. Gemma Rovira Ortega)
J. K. Rowling, *Harry Potter and the Goblet of Fire*
(*Harry Potter y el cáliz de fuego*, transl. Adolfo Muñoz García, Nieves Martín Azofra)
J. K. Rowling, *Harry Potter and the Half-Blood Prince*
(*Harry Potter y el misterio del príncipe*, transl. Gemma Rovira Ortega)
J. K. Rowling, *Harry Potter and the Order of the Phoenix*
(*Harry Potter y la Orden del Fénix*, transl. Gemma Rovira Ortega)
J. K. Rowling, *Harry Potter and the Philosopher's Stone*
(*Harry Potter y la piedra filosofal*, transl. Alicia Dellepiane)
J. K. Rowling, *Harry Potter and the Prisoner of Azkaban*
(*Harry Potter y el prisionero de Azkaban*, transl. Adolfo Muñoz García, Nieves Martín Azofra)
William Styron, *Sophie's choice*
(*La decisión de Sophie*, transl. Antoni Pigrau)
John R. R. Tolkien, *The Fellowship of the Ring*
(*La Comunidad del Anillo*, transl. Luis Domènech)
John. R. R. Tolkien, *The Hobbit*
(*El hobit*, transl. Manuel Figueroa)
John R. R. Tolkien, *The Return of the King*
(*El retorno del Rey*, transl. Luis Domènech, Matilde Holde)
John. R. R. Tolkien, *The Two Towers*
(*Las dos torres*, transl. Luis Domènech, Matilde Holde)